Keeping Up With Oracle Database 12c Multitenant

Book One

CDBs, PDBs and the Multitenant World

Part of The Keeping Up with Oracle Series

Robert G. Freeman

ISBN: 978-1507628157
ISBN-13: 1507628153

DEDICATION

This book is dedicated to my wonderful wife, Carrie and all of my children. You are all a wonderful inspiration and keep me nice and centered.

COPYRIGHT AND OTHER NOTICES

CONTENTS

INTRODUCTION

This book is the introductory book to the Keep Up With Oracle series. This series attempts to be the solution to a problem. Oracle Database continues to grow and add features with every release. The pace is dizzying. A normal book can take a year from beginning to end to get to press. By that time, the information in that book can be superseded by a new release of the database software. As a result, the book is aged before you even have an opportunity to buy it.. Enter the Keeping Up With Oracle series.

Another problem is that some books are just cannot be cost justified in the traditional printing world. Few publishers are interested in printing a book that will sell maybe 500 copies in the first year. Enter the Keeping Up With Oracle series. Our printing and delivery model is simple and much more inexpensive. Therefore we can tackle topics with a smaller audience.

At its heart, it is the goal of the Keeping Up With Oracle series to provide a new paradigm for technical books. Each book in the series will be focused on a specific area in the database. Individual books on this topic are kept smaller, with the overall subject matter will be covered in one or more books. The reason for this is to make it easier to update these books and keep them current. Instead of having to wait for the entire book to be updated, now, you the individual parts of the book will be updated and then brought to press as soon as possible.

This book is my first effort in this new paradigm of book production. In this book I'm tackling the new Multitenant features of the Oracle Database. This very powerful new feature of the Oracle Database, while remaining very familiar, also changes many of the old ways you manage databases. While Multitenant might not be big now, it will grow and quickly reach critical mass. Whether it's now or three years from now, most DBA's will be managing Oracle Multitenant databases eventually. Hopefully this book will help you in your transition to a Multitenant database DBA.

Robert G. Freeman – January 2015

ACKNOWLEDGMENTS

No book is ever written without a lot of help. Even with this attempt to self-publish there are still people to thank. Most of all, thanks to my wife. She read though this book and, when it wasn't boring her to death, she provided awesome feedback. Also, I want to just acknowledge everyone who has helped me to being at the point in my life that I can try this self-publishing thing. There are way too many people to name in that light.

1
INTRODUCTION TO ORACLE MULTITENANT

Oracle Database 12c introduced a completely revolutionary architecture called Oracle Multitenant. This architecture turns the concept of an Oracle database on its head. It is the goal of this book to introduce you to Oracle Multitenant. Now is a good time to learn about Oracle Multitenant because it is the wave of the future. It is where Oracle is going and you are right to want to learn about how it works.

In this chapter we will introduce you to Oracle Multitenant database. We will discuss the Oracle Multitenant Database architecture including the concepts of the Container Database(CDB) and the Pluggable Database (PDB). Then we will discuss CDBs and PDBs in much more detail.

Why Should I Care About Oracle Multitenant?

You may have looked at Oracle Multitenant and all of the wonderful new features it had. Then, you might have felt your heart drop a bit when you found that Multitenant was a licensed option – essentially you had to pay for it to be able to use it. As a result, you might have felt that there were better things to do with your time than learn about Oracle Multitenant. You might also have felt that there was no reason to use Multitenant, since you were not licensed. I would disagree, for several reasons.

First, there is a caveat to the licensing – you can actually use Oracle Multitenant in a limited way without any additional licensing. In this case you create a multitenant capable database (called a CDB, which we will discuss later in this book). Then you will create a single pluggable database (PDB – which we will discuss in more detail later) within the CDB you created. When you only have one PDB within a CDB, then no additional license is required. This means that you can actually run Oracle Multitenant enabled databases within your production database environment without additional licensing right now. Beyond this fact, I think there are a number of good reasons.

Also, you should look at **Oracle Multitenant as a glimpse into the future**. As such, it makes sense to expect that more and more that database features will be embracing the Multitenant architecture. Also, Oracle has just announced that the old Oracle architecture (called the non-CDB architecture) will eventually be de-supported. This reason alone should motivate you to embrace Multitenant.

1

In the Oracle DBA world, it's best not to get behind. Getting behind can be easy to do. Take, for example, Oracle Real Application Clusters (RAC) and how it's grown. If you are a DBA with a lot of past experience, then you can remember the days when RAC (or its predecessor Oracle Parallel Server) was really rare. Many DBA's didn't learn about how this feature of the database worked because they didn't see a reason to lean. Many DBA's didn't learn about how RAC worked because they didn't have the environments to learn in too.

However, the future has caught up with us, and all of a sudden RAC databases are everywhere. Those who had gotten on-board early and knew RAC didn't find this change impacting them at all. Those who didn't get on board found that things had moved and that all of a sudden job postings where RAC experience was a requirement were becoming more common. If you didn't know what **crsctl** was, much less how to start a node on a cluster, you were behind in the curve in a very negative way.

History is set to repeat itself with Multitenant Database. While adoption might be slow at the moment, I assure you that it is coming. In this case, Oracle has, in fact, told us that it's coming. Many people have complained about this, but all the complaining in the world isn't going to change the fact that Multitenant is going to be the way that Oracle goes in the future.

There are compelling operational reasons to move to the Multitenant architecture anyway. This is true even if it's using just a single PDB. For example, Multitenant simplifies the upgrade of databases. With even one database in a pluggable database environment, you can still take advantage of these features. Multitenant also has some very nice cloning features that simplify database cloning significantly, including between two separate CDB's. As time goes on and new features are added to Multitenant you can be sure that there will be even more arguments for moving to Multitenant.

If you have a license for Multitenant then Multitenant offers a number of features that can be of help to you as the DBA. We will be discussing many of these features in this book but here is short list of some of the more helpful features:

- You can consolidate your existing databases into one instance.
- Oracle Database is designed to efficiently manage the resources of a CDB and the PDB's attached to it.
  - One CDB with ten PDB's will make much better use of memory and CPU resources.

- o   Make the most of the resources you currently own, and reduce the number of resources that you need to procure in the future.
- Multitenant provides a number of features that will make cloning a database, or creating a new database from scratch much easier.
- Multitenant provides the ability to move databases easily between different CDB's.
- Multitenant makes upgrading PDB's quite easy and straightforward.
- Multitenant provides the ability to isolate PDB's completely from each other. Each PDB has its own accounts that are unique to that PDB.
- Multitenant provides the ability to manage the shared resources usage between PDB's.
- You can perform many different kinds of backups and restores on PDB's and CDB's with RMAN.
- Multitenant supports most Oracle Database features. There are a few features that are not yet supported, but that number has quickly decreased. Oracle's direction is that Multitenant will support all the features that Oracle Database Non-Multitenant will.
- Multitenant offers better adherence to standards, increasing uptime and reducing costs.
- Multitenant provides a much superior solution to schema consolidation.

All of that being said, now is a very good time to be concerned about learning about Oracle Multitenant.

The Oracle Multitenant Architecture

This section will introduce you to the Oracle Multitenant Architecture. The Oracle Multitenant Architecture is an optional architecture that is built on top of the Oracle Database that you already know. Therefore, there are many things about the architecture of Oracle Database that have not really changed at a high level. Certainly there are internal changes that have been made, but things like the SGA with its Buffer Cache, Shared Pool and other structures remain and are, in most cases, maintained the same way you have always maintained them. In this section we will introduce you to the two main components of this new architecture, the Container Database (CDB) and the Pluggable Database (PDB).

The Oracle Container Database (CDB)

When you create a database in Oracle Database 12*c* you have two different kinds of databases that you can create. The first, and default, option is to create the basic Oracle database. This is the same Oracle database architecture that you have used forever. The second is an option to create the database as a Container Database (CDB). The container database provides an architecture that allows more than one Oracle database to share the resources of a single database instance.

When an Oracle CDB is crated, the databases created within that CDB are called unique, and individually called Containers. When those containers are non-administrative databases, we called them Pluggable Databases (PDB's). Each PDB is completely isolated from every other PDB. We will discuss the security considerations of the CDB architecture in much more detail later in this book.

You create a CDB by including the **enable_pluggable_database** clause when issuing the **create database** command. If you are creating the database with the DBCA, then there is a checkbox option to create the database as a Multitenant database. You can also name the new PDB in a text box that the DBCA provides for you.

The CDB is much like an Oracle database in many respects. It can run as a single instance database, or it can be run as a Real Application Cluster (RAC) database, serving multiple database instances. The main ways a CDB differs from a normal Oracle database are

1. The CDB database instance can support more than one database (individually called PDB's).
2. The storage of most data dictionary information is stored locally in the individual PDB's and not the data dictionary of the CDB.

So, the CDB is no longer the main repository of database metadata. It has data dictionary like structures, and it also has views that provide information that are specific to the management of the CDB itself. A majority of the database metadata is stored at the PDB level though. All of that being said, the data dictionary has not changed a great deal and it will feel very familiar to you, even with the use of the PDB. We will discuss these changes in more detail, later in this book.

There are Five primary components within the Container database. These components include:

- The *Oracle Database instance* which provides the memory and process infrastructure that supports the Container Database.

- The *CDB database data dictionary* which maintains global information about the CDB and attached PDB's. The CDB data dictionary also contains views that provide real-time and historical performance information.

- The *ROOT container* of the CDB. Internally called CDB$ROOT. This container is created when the CDB is created and is critical to the operation of the CDB. The root container stores the data dictionary objects associated with the CDB.

- The *SEED container* of the CDB. Internally called PDB$SEED, this container is a static READ ONLY container (database) that contains a base set of objects that are used when creating a new Pluggable Database. The seed container provides for very fast creation of new PDB's.

- The *Pluggable database (PDB)*. Each individual database managed by the CDB is called a pluggable database. I will discuss PDB's in more detail shortly. Each PDB has its own local data dictionary.

Figure 1-1 Provides a general visualization of these five main components of a CDB.

Figure 1-1 Diagram of CDB Components

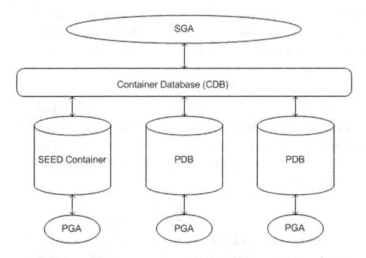

The database instance that runs the CDB is managed almost exactly like the database instances that you have been managing for years. Settings related to the CDB are managed through the use of a database SPFILE (or text parameter file if you prefer). It allocates the SGA and other memory areas just as any other database instance would. Note that all memory allocations of the SGA are at the CDB level and you do not allocate SGA memory to individual PDB's.

User processes can connect to the CDB or any PDB. As before, every connected user process will create its own PGA memory areas. There are a few considerations when configuring the parameters for a CDB. We will discuss these in more detail later when we discuss the creation of CDB's and PDB's.

While there is much logical separation between the CDB and it's child PDB's there are some critical components that are created in the CDB that all of the PDB's will use. This includes the UNDO tablespace as well as the SYSTEM and SYSAUX tablespaces of the CDB.

The CDB contains a single UNDO tablespace that serves all of the PDB's running in the CDB. As a result, when creating a PDB you need to be aware of how much UNTO tablespace you will need to manage the undo requirements of the PDB's that will be owned by that CDB. If you are running RAC, then there will be a single UNDO tablespace for each instance, just as there has always been. You cannot create an UNDO tablespace in an individual PDB. If you attempt to do so, an error will occur.

Both the CDB and any PDB's will have their own SYSTEM and SYSAUX tablespaces. This is something that is unique in the Multitenant architecture. Most PDB related metadata is stored locally in the PDB and the CDB data dictionary views simply have links that point to the metadata stored in the PDB.

Storing data dictionary information locally in the PDB facilitates quick cloning operations as well as being able to quickly plug-in or unplug a PDB. This book will talk about the data dictionary of the CDB and PDB in many places of course. Chapter 4 in this volume provides a more detailed look at how to use the various data dictionary views to manage CDB's and PDB's in Oracle Database 12c. Later books in this series will provide even more detailed information on the data dictionary and how to use it for a number of things including performance monitoring, tuning, security and other common DBA tasks.

A CDB has the standard SYS and other accounts (ie: SYSTEM, MDSYS, ORDSYS and so on) that are present in a normal database You should never create objects in the CDB unless Oracle support specifically tells you to do so. This is really just an extension of the idea that you should not create objects as SYS, and you should not create objects in the SYSTEM (or SYSAUX) tablespace. Now, the entirety of the CDB is off limits for any kind of monkey business. The CDB is for administration of the PDB's plugged into her.

Once exception to the rule that you never create anything in the CDB is that you will create a new kind of user in the CDB. This kind of user is called a common user. A common user is a user that can have various levels of access across the entire CDB and all of its PDB's. We will discuss common users in chapters 4 and 5 of this book.

Just in case you are skipping ahead a bit, you should know that you cannot create a regular account in a CDB. If you try to create a user account, for example ROBERT, in a CDB you will get the following error:

```
SQL> create user robert identified by admin_robert;
create user robert identified by admin_robert
        *

ERROR at line 1:
ORA-65096: invalid common user or role name
```

This is because you can only create common user accounts in the CDB. Be patient – we will get there. Common user accounts are very powerful, but they also take some management in order to get them to work just the way you want, without also giving away the keys to the kingdom.

Now that we have given you a quick look at CDB's, let's take a quick look at PDB's.

The Oracle Pluggable Database (PDB)

In this section I want to give you a quick overview of the Oracle PDB architecture. I am not going to deal with specific commands at this point, that will come later. What I want to do is give you a basic feel for what a PDB looks and feels like. Then, you will be better prepared to actually administer one.

First, a PDB is associated with a single CDB. A given CDB can have up to 252 PDB's contained in it. The PDB is, for all practical purposes, a self-contained database. It has its own name, identifier, DBID, guid and so on. Everything in the PDB is isolated from other PDB's and to a large extent even from the parent CDB.

Not all Oracle Databases can support PDB's. They have to have been created to do so. You can quickly query the V$DATABASE data dictionary view to determine if your database is able to create a PDB as seen in this example:

```
SQL> select cdb from v$database;

CDB
---
YES
```

In this case, our database is capable of hosting PDB's. This query would return a NO if the database was not created as a CDB, and therefore not able to host PDB's. You cannot modify a databases ability to support PDB's. If it cannot support a PDB and you want to use Multitenant, then you will need to re-create the database, or create a new CDB database and plug the non-CDB database into the newly created CDB database.

Perhaps one of the biggest differences with respect to Multitenant databases is that for non-administrative activity you must use a TNS connect string. This means that you can't connect to the PDB by setting the ORACLE_SID parameter in the environment. There is a method for administrators to connect to a PDB to perform administrative activities that does not require the use of Oracle networking. We will discuss all of this in much more detail throughout the book.

Note!

The requirement to use Oracle TNS Connection strings may require modification of scripts that currently connect by setting the ORACLE_SID environmental variable and then use SQL*Plus.

Each PDB has its own local administration accounts, including its own SYS account. As with non-CDB databases, you can create administrative accounts inside an individual PDB just like you would any other database. This allows for easy separation of duties, since the PDB administrator can only access specific PDB's they are assigned to. Of course, each PDB can have an account with the same name. I can have a ROBERT_ADMIN account in a PDB called PDBONE and a ROBERT_ADMIN account in a PDB called PDBTWO. So user account namespaces are unique at the PDB level.

The CDB, and each PDB, has their own separate set of data dictionary views. Both have the normal DBA, USER and ALL data dictionary views that you are used too. A new set of global data dictionary views have also been added called the CDB views. The CDB views provide global access across all PDB's within the CDB to an administrator account with the appropriate privileges. We will discuss the data dictionary and various dictionary views throughout the chapter of this book, and the other books of the series.

Creating and Dropping PDB's
Creating and removing PDB's is fairly simple work. In this section we will briefly discuss the different ways that you can create and remove PDB's. We will also discuss some issues that you will want to be aware of when you perform these operations. Later in this book, we will go into detail on how to create PDB's from the SQL command line. In the next book in this

series we will discuss other ways of creating PDB's including plugging and unplugging them. For now, let's quickly look at the different methods that can be sued to create and remove PDB's.

Methods of Creating PDB's

There are many ways of creating PDB's which include the following:

- Using the **create pluggable database** command to create the PDB while connected to the CDB.
- Using the **create pluggable database** command to plug an existing PDB into the CDB.
- Using the DBCA utility following a guided workflow.
- Using Oracle Cloud Control to guide you through the creation of the PDB.
- Cloning an existing PDB to a new PDB with, or without data.
- Creating an empty PDB and using Oracle Data Pump to import data from one database source into a PDB.

Each of these ways of creating a PDB comes with its own set of rules and unique options and features. We will cover each of these as we progress through this book, and the later books of this series.

When a PDB is created from scratch (for example, by using the **create pluggable database** SQL command) it will have its own unique SYSTEM, SYSAUX and TEMPORARY tablespaces. Once the PDB is created, you can create other tablespaces within the PDB as needed. The visibility of a tablespace is local to that PDB – this makes it possible for every PDB to have tablespaces that are named the same. This also means that all of the data in a PDB is isolated to that PDB.

When the PDB is created a TNS network service is created that will support the new PDB. This service will also register with the database listener process so that you can access the PDB through its service name. The default service name is the same as the PDB, and you can create additional service names too. If fact, Oracle recommends that you not use the default service name, and that you create new service names for security purposes.

Methods of Removing PDB's

There are also several ways that you can remove PDB's. These include:

- The SQL prompt, using the **drop pluggable database** command.
- Using the DBCA utility following a guided workflow to remove a PDB.
- Using Oracle Enterprise Manager Cloud Control to remove the PDB
- Unplugging the PDB
- Deleting the entire CDB.

All of these options will be covered in much greater detail in this and later books of this series.

Keeping PDB's Unique

If we are going to have several PDB's in our CDB (and our database server and it's physical storage) then it's clear that there must be some way to keep these PDB's separated both logically and physically. In this section we are going to discuss how Oracle performs this separation. First we will look at how PDB's are separated at a logical level. Then we will look at how PDB's are segregated at a physical level.

Keeping PDB's Logically Unique

Given that a CDB can host many PDB's (and that a physical server can host many CDB's), there must be a way that Oracle uses to avoid collisions with the physical files in the database. There are several things that make the PDB unique. First is the name of the PDB itself. Within a given CDB, each PDB must be named uniquely. This makes sense as it avoids problems like collision with service names and the like.

Within the data dictionary views of the CDB there is column that represents a unique ID for the container/PDB within that CDB. This new column is called CONT_ID column in data CDB and PDB dictionary views. This column can be found in a number of data dictionary views that helps you to identify which container owns which object. You will see examples of the use of the CONT_ID column throughout the books in this series.

Next, each PDB has a Global Unique Identifier (GUID) that is assigned to it. The GUID is generated when the PDB is created. The GUID is designed to be a globally unique identifier for that PDB, which helps avoid various types of collisions. For example, the GUID is used as part of the default directory path for the storage of the physical datafiles that belong to a PDB. The GUID then physical separation and isolation for the datafiles belonging to an individual PDBs. This is preferable to using the CON_ID identifier instead as it would be very likely that a given CON_ID would be repeated on given server with more than one CDB. Also, if you move a PDB from one server to another, the possibility of CON_ID collisions is much higher than that of GUID collisions.

Clearly, using the GUID, with its assured uniqueness, eliminates the risk of PDB related namespace collisions. So, you can see that the GUID is not only used to logically make the PDB distinct, but that it's also used to make the files associated with the PDB distinct on the physical layer (by default – this can always be overridden of course).

> **Warning!**
>
> **OFA uses the GUID of the PDB as a part of the physical file naming structure. We have seen that some DBA's new to the CDB/PDB architecture decide to change this standard and not use the GUID (usually because it's a long and unruly number). I strongly recommend that you stick to the OFA standard, including the use of the GUID.**

Both the container ID and the GUID of the PDB's can be seen through querying the data dictionary view V$PDBS. In the following query we see the NAME, CON_ID and GUID of each PDB currently plugged into the database.

The following example shows how you can query the V$PDBS view to get the name, container id and guid of the PDBs in your database:

```
SQL> select name, con_id, guid from v$pdbs;

NAME                            CON_ID GUID
------------------------------- ------ ------------------------
PDB$SEED                             2 D833A154A42A480CA35CF076F630A5BA
ROBERTPDB                            3 379B3D1EDF1449C48BC625D5DA102859
TPLUG                                4 0EA6466993554DD393A7DE69001594A1
```

In this output we see that this CDB has three PDB's. The first is the seed container (PDB) called PDB$SEED. The PDB$SEED container is created when the database is first created. It's function is to provide a source from which to create new PDBs.

After the SEED PDB, notice that we have two other PDB's:

ROBERTPDB and TPLUG. You can see that each PDB has a unique CON_ID associated with it. Also notice the GUID column in the output and that each GUID is unique.

There is also the view V$CDBS which presents us with an additional row as seen here:

SQL> select name, con_id, guid from v$containers;

```
NAME                    CON_ID GUID
------------------- ------ --------------------------------
CDB$ROOT                 1 01685D864667499897328284C5680FFA
PDB$SEED                 2 D833A154A42A480CA35CF076F630A5BA
ROBERTPDB                3 379B3D1EDF1449C48BC625D5DA102859
TPLUG                    4 0EA6466993554DD393A7DE69001594A1
```

This view adds what we call the root container, CDB$ROOT. You can see that the ROOT container didn't show up in the first view, but it did show up in the second view.

This is going to be one of the main learning curves that you will have in your effort to understand how Multitenant works. Since there is a new layer to deal with in the database (CDB vs. PDB) there are a number of new rules related to security which impacts what you can see when querying data dictionary views. Don't worry though – we will cover all of these things throughout the books of this series.

Within the Multitenant architecture, there are some objects that are shared by all of the PDB's, and there are some things that are not. Recall the main physical components of a database:

- Datafiles
- Online redo logs
- Control files
- SPFILE or Parameter file

Of this list, the datafiles are the only non-shared physical component in a Multitenant database. Each tablespace in each PDB has its own set of datafiles unique to that PDB. However the remaining objects are shared across the entire Multitenant database. For example, all of the redo generated by all of the PDB's is stored in the database online redo logs. There are no online redo logs dedicated to any particular PDB. This might mean if you have (or will have) several databases into your CDB that you will have to size the redo log files accordingly.

Also, recall some of the tablespace objects in an Oracle Database:

- SYSTEM tablespace
- SYSAUX tablespace
- UNDO tablespace
- Temporary tablespaces
- User tablespaces

Each PDB has its own SYSTEM, SYSAUX, and also its own temporary tablespace. Also, each PDB may have its own user defined tablespaces. The one thing that is different is that the only UNDO tablespace you will have is owned by the ROOT container (if you are running RAC then you will have one UNDO tablespace per instance).

Keeping PDB's Physically Separated

Logical separation of PDB's is just one issue that needs to be addressed by the Oracle database to avoid namespace collisions. Physical separation of database datafiles (the only real physical files that risk namespace collisions) associated with PDB's is very important. Since it is possible that a given PDB might have the same datafile names as a PDB that is being imported (or as a new tablespace is being created). By default, Oracle uses the Oracle Managed Files (OMF) feature to assure that files are properly separated. While OMF can be overridden by the DBA when tablespaces are created, in most cases I would strongly recommended that you allow OMF to place and name your files for you.

The typical file placement convention begins with either the configuration of the DB_CREATE_FILE_DEST parameter, or with the assignment of the tablespace to be created to an ASM disk group. In both cases, Oracle will put the datafiles associated with the CDB Database and the SEED PDB in the same directory. Under this base directory unique directories are created for each PDB using the GUID of that PDB for the directory name. Under these directories, OMF creates directories for the types of files to be stored, such a datafiles. In these directories, Oracle stores the appropriate database files.

As an example, let's look at a database called ROBERTCDB. This database is using file systems to store it's datafiles. The parameter DB_CREATE_FILE_DEST is set to a value of /u01/app/oracle/oradata. Under the oradata directory, since we are using OMF, Oracle will create additional directories as required. In our case it has created a directory called /u01/app/oracle/oradata/. In the following code listings, we will explore this directory and see where Oracle has put our datafiles. If we look on the database server at the location defined by the parameter DB_CREATE_FILE_DEST we will find that a directory was created by the Oracle database for our database. It is called ROBERTCDB. Below that directory we have a number of other directories as seen in this listing:

```
[oracle@bigdatalite ROBERTCDB]$ pwd
/u01/app/oracle/oradata/ROBERTCDB
[oracle@bigdatalite ROBERTCDB]$ ls -al
total 28
drwxr-x---.  7 oracle oinstall 4096 Jan 7 15:17 .
drwxrwxr-x. 15 oracle oinstall 4096 Dec 9 17:59 ..
drwxr-x---.  3 oracle oinstall 4096 Jan 7 15:17
0C16988CADC77D93E0530100007F18D4
drwxr-x---.  2 oracle oinstall 4096 Dec 9 18:13 controlfile
drwxr-x---.  2 oracle oinstall 4096 Dec 9 18:20 datafile
drwxr-x---.  2 oracle oinstall 4096 Dec 9 18:14 onlinelog
```

The directories controlfile, datafile and online log are the directories that store the physical files for the CDB and the SEED database. For example, if we change into the datafile directory, we will find these files (I've modified the output to make it easier to read on many of the directory listings you will see in this book):

```
[oracle@bigdatalite datafile]$ pwd
/u01/app/oracle/oradata/ROBERTCDB/datafile
[oracle@bigdatalite ROBERTCDB]$ cd datafile
[oracle@bigdatalite datafile]$ ls -al
total 2501304
o1_mf_sysaux_bb3q6oym_.dbf
o1_mf_sysaux_bb3r406o_.dbf
o1_mf_system_bb3qkkbv_.dbf
o1_mf_system_bb3r407g_.dbf
o1_mf_temp_bb3r31nd_.tmp
o1_mf_undotbs1_bb3qyf38_.dbf
o1_mf_users_bb3qy8qb_.dbf
pdbseed_temp012014-12-29_06-20-16-PM.dbf
```

Here we find two SYSTEM, SYSAUX tablespace datafiles, one for the CDB and one for the SEED database. Also we find the other tablespace datafiles. Such as temp, undotbs2 and so on. We can see these datafiles in the V$DATAFILE data dictionary view just like we can in a non-Multitenant database as seen in this SQL code output (this is only a partial bit of the output):

```
select a.con_id, c.name CDB_NM, a.name TBS_NAME, b.name
from v$tablespace a, v$datafile b, v$containers c
where a.ts#=b.TS#
and a.con_id=b.con_id
and c.con_id=a.con_id
order by 1;

CON_ID CDB_NM    TBS_NAME
------ ---------- ----------------
NAME
-----------------------------------------------------------------
     1 CDB$ROOT    SYSTEM
/u01/app/oracle/oradata/ROBERTCDB/datafile/
o1_mf_system_bb3qkkbv_.dbf
     1 CDB$ROOT    SYSAUX
/u01/app/oracle/oradata/ROBERTCDB/datafile/
o1_mf_sysaux_bb3q6oym_.dbf
     1 CDB$ROOT    UNDOTBS1
/u01/app/oracle/oradata/ROBERTCDB/datafile/
o1_mf_undotbs1_bb3qyf38_.dbf
     1 CDB$ROOT    USERS
/u01/app/oracle/oradata/ROBERTCDB/datafile/
o1_mf_users_bb3qy8qb_.dbf
     2 PDB$SEED    SYSTEM
/u01/app/oracle/oradata/ROBERTCDB/datafile/
o1_mf_system_bb3r407g_.dbf
     2 PDB$SEED    SYSAUX
/u01/app/oracle/oradata/ROBERTCDB/datafile/
o1_mf_sysaux_bb3r406o_.dbf
     3 ROBERTPDB   SYSTEM
/u01/app/oracle/oradata/ROBERTCDB/0C16988CADC77D93E0530100007F18D4/
datafile/o1_mf_system_bbv52nvv_.dbf
     3 ROBERTPDB   SYSAUX
/u01/app/oracle/oradata/ROBERTCDB/0C16988CADC77D93E0530100007F18D4/
datafile/o1_mf_sysaux_bbv52nxo_.dbf
```

Notice that I displayed both the CON_ID column and the name of the associated PDB. This is to point out a couple of things. First, in a given CDB, each container has a CON_ID assigned to it. You can find the CON_ID and the name of the container it is associated with by querying the V$PDBS view as we did earlier in this chapter. All of the V$ views that contain metadata related to PDB's contain data about all of the PDB's.

How PDB related metadata is handled differs between the V$ views and the DBA views. Keep in mind that the V$ views (dynamic data dictionary views) normally source from the control file or some specific internal structures that are created when the database instance is started.

The data dictionary views (those that typically start with DBA, USER ALL and now the new CDB views) source from various metadata in the database data dictionary. With respect to multitenant databases, that includes data dictionary information in those PDB's. Remembering where the data dictionary data comes from will help you as you come to understand why information is reported differently in the dynamic and data dictionary views of a CDB.

For example, suppose you query the CDB_TABLES view, looking for tables for a PDB called TEST. Assume then that the query returns no rows. Now, you know there are a ton of tables in the TEST PDB. Given your knowledge about where the metadata from the CDB_TABLES view comes from, what might be one reason that there are no rows returned? One very possible reason might be that the PDB is not open. If the PDB is not open, it can't be queried about its data dictionary information and thus the CDB_TABLES query will return no rows for that PDB.

Moving on, let's look at the listing of the directory where the ROBERCDB datafiles are located (/u01/app/oracle/oradata/ROBERTCDB) again (again, I've cut the directory listing output to make it easier to read):

```
[oracle@bigdatalite ROBERTCDB]$ pwd
/u01/app/oracle/oradata/ROBERTCDB
[oracle@bigdatalite ROBERTCDB]$ ls -al
total 28
drwxr-x---.   oracle oinstall 4096 Jan   7 15:17 .
drwxrwxr-x.   oracle oinstall 4096 Dec 29 17:59 ..
drwxr-x---.   0C16988CADC77D93E0530100007F18D4
drwxr-x---.   controlfile
drwxr-x---.   datafile
drwxr-x---.   onlinelog
```

Notice the directory named 0C16988CADC77D93E0530100007F18D4? That is the directory where the datafiles associated with a PDB in our database are stored. The directory name is the GUID of the PDB, so now you can see one reason why it's important for the GUID to be unique. Recall from earlier in this chapter, that you can find the PDB that the GUID is associated with from the V$PDBS view as seen in this example:

```
SQL> select name, guid from v$pdbs where
guid='0C16988CADC77D93E0530100007F18D4'

NAME                          GUID
----------------------        ------------------------------
ROBERTPDB                     0C16988CADC77D93E0530100007F18D4
```

So now we can see that the data in this directory is likely owned by the

ROBERTPDB PDB. I say likely because you can override where datafiles get created (so always cross check what you believe to be true against the data dictionary views of the CDB). It's important to realize that the PDB datafiles are only created in the GUID based directory by default. It's very possible to have a particular file located elsewhere, and not in that directory. Therefore, it's always a good idea to cross-check the data dictionary before you go looking for physical files and assuming they are in this directory (have I said that enough times now that you won't forget?)

> **Warning!**
>
> **In the case of PDBs that have been copied from another CDB it is very possible that the datafiles for that PDB may still reside in the datafile structure of the old CDB. Use caution when cleaning what might appear to be unneeded files from a directory.**

Now, let's go look at what is in the GUID based directory. First, when we traverse into the this directory we find another directory called datafiles. In that directory we find the three files associated with the ROBERPDB PDB. Here is the directory listing:

```
[oracle@bigdatalite datafile]$ pwd
/u01/app/oracle/oradata/ROBERTCDB/
0C16988CADC77D93E0530100007F18D4/datafile

[oracle@bigdatalite datafile]$ ls -al
total 757848
drwxr-x---. 2 oracle oinstall     4096 Jan  7 15:19 .
drwxr-x---. 3 oracle oinstall     4096 Jan  7 15:17 ..
-rw-r-----.  ol_mf_sysaux_bbv52nxo_.dbf
-rw-r-----.  ol_mf_system_bbv52nvv_.dbf
-rw-r-----.  ol_mf_temp_bbv52ny5_.dbf
```

These files appeared in the query against the V$DATAFILES view that we demonstrated earlier. So, the files appear to be where they are supposed to be!

Note that all of these files that we have looked at are the files for pretty much the most basic CDB/PDB that can be created. As you add PDB's, and as you add various datafiles to those PDB's (or add them to the CDB to expand the size of its tablespaces) it's important to follow some form of naming standard to avoid trouble. My experience has shown that when you are trying to free up space, it's way too easy to find a file that is out in the middle of nowhere on your file system. You look at things a bit and decide that it's not being used, and you remove it. Of course, that is when the phone calls come and you discover that you really should not have removed that file. This is also where great tools like **lsof** come in handy!

Summary

In this chapter I introduced you to Oracle Multitenant. First, we discussed some of the reasons why you should care about Multitenant in the first place, even if you are not licensed for it. Then we took a look at the Oracle Multitenant architecture where we introduced you to the CDB and the PDB. Coming up next we will talk about how to create a CDB, so that you can then start creating PDB's.

2
CREATING THE CDB

Now that you have learned the fundamentals of a Multitenant database, let's discuss the creation of one. In reality, the creation of a CDB is not unlike the creation of a non-CDB database. To create the CDB you will use either the Oracle Database Configuration Assistant (DBCA) or the **create database** command. In this book, we will focus on using the DBCA. If you want to use the **create database** command then please refer to the Oracle documentation.

There are several steps involved in the creation of an Oracle CDB with the DBCA. While these steps are similar to the creation of a non CDB, there are some special considerations that you will want to be aware of. Also, I will provide what I think are some best practices to follow when creating a CDB. Finally, keep in mind that when you are creating the CDB that there will be one or more PDB's that you will create too. This might impact your planning of things like memory configuration or physical placement of datafiles.

In this chapter we have divided the creation of the PDB into these three steps:

- Pre-database creation activities
- Database Creation
- Post-database creation activities

Let's look at each of these in more detail next.

Note!

Obviously a single chapter in a book cannot be considered a complete checklist. You should carefully review the Oracle documentation if you are not familiar with the requirements of creating a non-Multitenant database. In this chapter we are only highlighting the things that are specific to the creation of a CDB in preparation for the creation of PDB's within it.

Pre-database Creation Activities
Before you start creating your CDB there are several tasks that should be

completed to ensure the database is both created correctly and successfully. We are going to assume that you have already installed the Oracle Database software. You will use the same database software as if you are creating a non-CDB database, so there is nothing special there. After the software is installed, you are ready to create databases.

One thing to keep in mind while configuring a CDB is that you are configuring an environment that will likely support more than one PDB. This impacts memory sizing, UNDO tablespace sizing, and online redo logs sizing, perhaps significantly. Also, you need to carefully consider configuration items that will impact the whole of the CDB. For example the database character set of a CDB becomes the character set for all PDB's in that database. Choosing the wrong character set can be a big deal.

Warning!

The importance of carefully selecting the character set that you will be using cannot be understated. First, the process of changing character sets is not an easy one. Second, during character set conversions it is possible to lose data if the existing character set is not compatible with the one you are converting too. Third, all of the PDB's in a given CDB must have the same character set.

So, let's talk about what we want to do before we create the CDB. In this section we have classified these tasks as:

- Determining the CDB name
- Determining where to put the files for the CDB and how big to make them
- Determining memory requirements for the CDB
- Determining the character set for the CDB
- Other parameters that require additional consideration with CDB's.

Let's look at these in a bit more detail.

Determine the CDB Name

Each CDB must have its own unique name on a given server. Frankly, I believe that with rare exceptions that CDB's should be unique through the entire enterprise.

There are different arguments for and against using some descriptive metadata to name a CDB. For example, if you intend on putting all of your test databases in the CDB, then you might want to call the CDB test. This certainly identifies the use of the CDB. However, I am not a big fan of this kind of naming scheme in an Enterprise environment. I would recommend that a smarter naming convention for a CDB would be nondescript. Why do I say this? There are several reasons:

Naming the CDB for the kind of PDB's it contains might be confusing. For example, you might initially plan to only store test databases on your CDB, and so you call it something imaginative like TEST. However, in the future you might also include PDBs that are for development and QA, along with testing. So, is TEST really the right name for that CDB? So, planning for the future is one reason I use nondescript CDB names.

Name collisions are a possibility. It might be that you will create a second CDB for test databases. Are you going to call it TEST1? What if you consolidate servers and all of a sudden you have two TEST CDB's? While there are ways to work around these issues, using a non-descriptive SID for the database can reduce these issues.

Perhaps the biggest argument for non-descript CDB (and PDB) names is security. In the day and age where hackers are real, and the risks are real, you don't want to provide anyone with any more information than you have to. When you name a CDB PROD, and it's the only one out of six CDB's in your enterprise a hacker knows about – which CDB do you think they are going to try to crack? If I have some non-descriptive SID for the CDB, this offers me some protection from prying eyes.

So, what do I suggest for a secure naming standard? I suggest that you simply use a random set of 8 characters for your SID. The randomness will eliminate any descriptiveness of the SID. The reason I suggest 8 is that this is the maximum size for a SID that Oracle recommends. While more characters might make it harder for you to remember names of SIDs in your mind, it will also make it harder for hackers to guess at those names.

Determining Where to put CDB files and Sizing them Correctly

Before you create your CDB, you will need to carefully consider where you will put your datafiles, and how you will size them. In this section I will address testing the performance of the file system you are planning on using for your database files. Then we will address where to put database related files, and how to size them correctly.

File System Performance

One important consideration to preparing for any database is to ensure that the file system you have configured, performs as expected and required. In Oracle Database 12c, Oracle has started shipping it's Orion tool. Orion can be used to test the performance of your file system with varying types of writes and concurrency. The results of Orion will provide you with information on IOPS, MBPS and latency rates on your file system. This is not a book on performance tuning, so I am not going to spend a lot of time on Orion. However, I thought I'd mention it. Orion is fully covered in the Oracle Database documentation. In particular I'd recommend that you review Chapter 4 of the Oracle High Availability Guide for information on configuring storage.

The correct configuration of storage is critical to a database that performs. Many clients that I have been involved with, who have performance problems, have not correctly configured something with respect to their storage infrastructure. DBA's need to be aware of how critical storage is, and how critical the correct storage infrastructure is. Storage administrators need to understand the storage footprint of databases better, so that they can create storage infrastructures that adequately support the IO needs of an Oracle Database.

Also, keep in mind that the "disks" are not the only part of the storage equation. The feeds and speeds of the connections between the disks and the database are also critical components. If your Fibre Channel card can only handle 850Mb/s, who cares if your disk system, with all that expensive flash in front of it can spit out data at 4000Mb/s? Just remember, it's the whole system and as Mr. Scott once said, "The more they over think the plumbing the easier it is to stop up the drain". No truer words have been spoken.

Datafile Location

It is important to determine a standard, with respect to the location of datafiles, associated with the CDB that you are creating. Oracle provides a set of best practices with respect to database storage. These recommendations are called the database high availability best practices and are documented in the book *Oracle Database 12c High Availability* that is available in the Oracle documentation set.

In Chapter 4 of the Oracle Database 12 High Availability book you will find a recommendation on how to allocate storage. The overall recommendation is to use a method called Stripe and Mirror Everything (SAME) when defining database storage. The SAME method of allocating storage provides the best method of storing data on physical media. Figure 2-1 provides an example of a 10-disk array that is configured using a SAME methodology.

In figure 2-1, you will see that 2 ASM file systems are created over a set of five disks. The other five disks are used to mirror those ASM file systems. You will see that all of the data in the ASM disk groups is striped across the two sets of five disks. This configuration provides a number of benefits including:

- High availability. The loss of one disk will not cause any loss of data or database availability. With ASM, the loss of a disk will also cause the data that was on the disk to be copied to surviving blocks in the disk group that disk belonged too, as long as space is available. In this way, you are further protected from the loss of additional disks after the copies are complete.

- Data protection. In the event of disk failure, or even block failure, ASM will copy the lost or corrupted data from the surviving mirrored disk.

- Flexible and scalable. It's easy to expand disk groups, add disks or move disks between disk groups all while the disk groups remain online.

- Provides higher I/O bandwidths because you are spreading the I/O over a larger number of disk spindles. This is a key consideration when dealing with databases.

- You can store data in a more finite manner. Thus, you can store database files on the faster part of the disk platters and files that don't require as much performance, such as backup files, can be stored on the less performant part of the disk.

- Support for copy on write technologies. These technologies support Oracle's ability to do fast cloning of PDB's.

Figure 2-1 Sample Disk Array Configured for ASM Using SAME

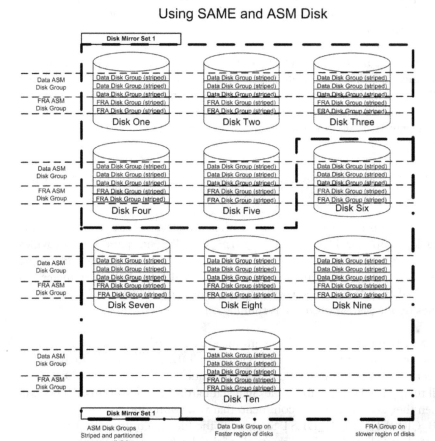

I strongly recommend that you allow your Oracle Databases to use OMF for datafile naming and placement. This provides a single standard that your enterprise can apply to the naming and placement of database datafiles. In many of a clients I've seen in the past, I very often find that there are no consistent standards employed with respect to datafile placement or naming.

While dealing with physical storage is a typical database administration, or even disk administrator responsibility and not specific to Multitenant Oracle you might wonder why I decided to include information on allocating storage.

Many Multitenant databases that will be created are going to be on new hardware. As such, you want to make sure you allocate the disk space in the most performant way. Performance is critical and very often the problems I find with respect to performance often are partly due to poor disk infrastructures.

Once you have created your file system or ASM disk group, much of the placement of database related files can, and should be, automated. Some DBA's just like to do their own thing – the problem is that in an enterprise doing your own thing does not work very well. Therefore, take advantage of the standards that the Oracle database itself provides.

When you are using ASM, Oracle creates all of the directories, and names all of the files, for you automatically. So, the best advice I can give you there is not to override ASM. Let it do its thing.

When you are using file systems, then we should start with setting the Oracle parameter DB_CREATE_FILE_DEST. This parameter provides the base directory that Oracle will start creating database related files. The default setting for the DB_CREATE_FILE_DEST parameter is $ORACLE_BASE/oradata/{database name} on Linux, and this value varies by the platform Oracle is running on.

When you create your CDB with the DBCA you will have the opportunity to set this parameter. Then, the DBCA will create the base directory structure for you along with all required sub-directories. DBCA will then place your database files in a standardized form on that file system when they are created. I recommend that you configure DB_CREATE_FILE_DEST to point to the file system that you have created and allow Oracle to create all of the database files using the standard it employs.

Datafile Sizes

What size should you make your datafiles? Oracle provides guidance on this, and I don't just want to repeat what they have to say. However, there are some things that I thought I should say with respect to datafile sizing:

First, make sure that **autoextend** is enabled for the SYSTEM tablespace of the CDB. I would also recommend that you enable **autoextend** on the SYSAUX and UNDO tablespaces. By default **autoextend** is enabled for the all of the tablespaces of the CDB when it is created by the DBCA. You might want to disable **autoextend** for the temporary tablespace, after making sure it's sized properly. This prevents bad SQL from causing the tablespace to grow without constraint. In development environments you will want to constrain growth of user tablespaces by setting a limit on how big these tablespaces can grow.

Even more important, make sure that the **next** value is properly set for SYSTEM, SYSAUX and any user created tablespaces that are likely to experience growth. The default value of **next** with respect to **autoextend** defaults to an incredibly small size when a tablespace is created. This causes problems when tablespace extensions occur because of the locking and significant database activity that occurs when the database had to extend a datafile. If the **next** size is very small, then the database is going to be adding space to datafiles almost constantly once you hit the allocated limit of the datafiles.. This can cause serious performance problems. For example, the SYSTEM tablespace increments a total of 1280 bytes by default. If your block size is 8k, that means you will need several datafile extensions to support just the addition of one block.

Normally the default datafile sizes that DBCA will create for, system realted tablespaces, are sufficient if properly supplemented with **autoextend** and a correctly set **next** value.

Much of this advice applies tablespaces that will contain user data too. The initial size of the datafile and settings for **next** and **autoextend** are critical. I also strongly advise using bigfile tablespaces. Managing one datafile for a tablespace is generally much easier. RMAN now supports section size backups, so you can now backup a bigfile tablespace much easier. Certainly, there may be reasons not to use bigfile tablespaces in your environment, but I'd make that the exception, not the rule.

> **Note!**
>
> **Keep in mind that when you are creating the CDB, the tablespaces of the CDB are not where a majority of your storage is going to take place. The vast majority of your storage will be consumed by the PDB's. You should never need to create new tablespaces in the CDB itself, and the need to add space to the standard tablespaces like SYSTEM and SYS should not be that frequent.**

Sizing Redo Logs

One common reason for performance problems is inadequate sizing of the online redo logs. By default the DBCA will create three online redo log groups, each with two members. The default size of the redo log members is 52 Megabytes in size. For any but the most boring of databases, this size is way too small. So, the question is, now big do you make them then? For a new CDB the answer depends on the number of PDB's you are going to use. Each PDB is going to create its own rate of redo. As we add PDB's to a CDB, the redo that will pass through the online redo logs is going to increase.

Sizing Redo for a Known Database

If you know which databases you are going to convert into PDB's, then you can look at the redo generation rate in those databases by using the data dictionary views of those databases. First, in general we want to see log switches occur every 10 to 15 minutes. This is because any faster than that can impact performance and any slower can impact recoverability. The amount of time that you should configure between switches can vary on a number of factors. These factors would include:

- The speed of the hardware (disk, CPU, etc) being used.
- Tolerance for data loss. The more time you allow between log switches, the more risk of data loss you face. So, there is a balance between performance gained by reducing the number of log switches and recoverability.

First and foremost, Oracle has the V$INSTANCE_RECOVERY view that provides the redo log advisor's information. The column OPTIMAL_LOG FILE_SIZE displays the suggestion of the redo log advisor on how large you should make the redo logs. This suggestion is based on the setting of the FAST_START_MTTR_RECOVERY parameter. This parameter indicates to Oracle the maximum amount of time that you want to have to spend on database instance recovery in the event of an instance crash. The higher the number, the more time instance recovery will be. The lower the number, Oracle will try to manage the system to minimize instance recovery time. Mainly the way this is done is through adjusting the velocity in which dirty buffers are flushed to disk. Faster instance recovery times demand flushing dirty buffers to disk more frequently. This is because one of the main determinants of how long instance recovery is will be how much redo has to be applied to the database datafiles before Oracle can open the database.

FAST_START_MTTR_RECOVERY has a default value of 0, and as a result the redo log advisor will not be running. If FAST_START_MTTR_RECOVERY was not set and you decide to set it, you will want to let your database run for a few days to ensure that the redo log advisor is giving you correct advice.

If you would like to look at historical data to cross check the recommendation of the redo advisor you can use views such as V$LOG_HISTORY. These views can provide some idea of how frequently log file switches are occurring in your database per day. For example, the results of this query will show us how many log switches occurred each day for the last 30 days:

```
select to_char(first_time, 'mm/dd/yyyy') round_date,
count(*) spd
from v$log_history
where first_time>=sysdate-30
group by to_char(first_time, 'mm/dd/yyyy')
order by 1 desc;
```

Looking at some sample output we find the following:

```
ROUND_DATE            SPD
----------  -----------------
12/31/2014             15
12/30/2014             27
01/09/2015             41
01/08/2015             35
01/07/2015              6
01/06/2015              9
01/05/2015             22
```

Now, if you had a log switch every 15 minutes, which is a general target I recommend, then that would be a total of 96 log switches per day. In this database, we find that we have much fewer log switches than that. In this case, we might want to investigate if the online redo logs are too large, because we are not switching enough. It might also be that this database has irregular activity and sits idle for a long period of time, each database is different. Another query that might be helpful in determining redo log utilization is seen here:

Note!

All of the recommendations and guidelines in this book are just that, recommendations and guidelines. These are very general in their nature and you have to ensure that they work for you – there is rarely one answer that holds true for all things.

```
with time_between as
(select  first_time,
lag(first_time,1) over (order by first_time) last_time,
(first_time   -   lag(first_time,1)    over    (order    by
first_time))*1440 time_between_min
from v$log_history )
select round(avg(time_between_min),2) avg_lg_swtch_tm_mn
,round(stddev(time_between_min),2) stnd_dev_time
from time_between;
```

and some sample results:

```
-- Run on DB 1
AVG_LG_SWTCH_TM_MN STND_DEV_TIME
------------------ -------------
           357.71         546.05

-- Run on DB 2
AVG_LG_SWTCH_TM_MN STND_DEV_TIME
------------------ -------------
            24.71           6.0
```

In the output in this example you will see that we are looking at all of the records in V$LOG_HISTORY and determining the amount of time between each log switch. Then we are calculating and displaying the average time between log switches. We have included a calculation of the standard deviation of the row set also, to give you an idea of how representative of real life that average value really is.

In the first case, we have an average time between log switches of 357 minutes, which is quite a lot. If we look at the standard deviation number, we see it's very high. This indicates that there is a lot of deviation from this average number. In other words, the average number is not very representative of any kind of trend. On the second example notice that our average log switches is every 24 minutes and the standard deviation is quite a bit lower. This would imply that the average number here is somewhat more consistent.

If you want to take a different look at redo generation, we can look at the historical generation over time and determine the approximate size of our log files. This query goes against the data dictionary tables in Oracle that store historical database information:

```
set numf 999,999,999.99
with redo_per_hour as (
select min(begin_time), max(end_time),
       round(max(end_time)-min(begin_time),2) days_snap,
       round(avg(value*(60*15)),2) avg_mb_redo_per_15,
       stddev(value) stddev_value
                      from dba_hist_sysmetric_history
                      where metric_id=2016),
log_data as (select max(bytes) log_bytes from v$log)
select b.days_snap days, b.avg_mb_redo_per_fifteen,
b.stddev_value,
a.log_bytes, a.log_bytes-b.avg_mb_redo_per_fifteen
ps_ovr_ng_under
from log_data a, redo_per_hour b;
```

DAYS	AVG_MB_REDO_PER_15	STDDEV_VALUE	LOG_BYTES	PS_OVR_NG_UNDER
7.24	881,877.16	11,109.68	52,428,800.00	51,546,922.84

In this query we see that there are seven days of history currently being stored in the view DBA_HIST_SYSMETRIC_HISTORY. The average redo generation every 15 minutes (again, my general benchmark) is listed. The Standard deviation is listed too. This particular database is often down for many days, so there are large gaps in time in the records. This is why the standard deviation is so high in this case. Then, we see the size of the redo log in the LOG_BYTES column. The final column shows us how oversized (or undersized) the redo logs are based on the average redo generation rate. In this case, the online redo logs are much bigger than the average amount of redo that is generated every fifteen minutes. So, it might make sense to reclaim some space and allocate a smaller amount of log space on your CDB for that database.

Let's circle back to the question of sizing the online redo logs of your CDB. You will need to go through each database that you will be moving to the new CDB and determine what it's redo generation rate is for whatever period of time that you want to see log switches occur. For example, if database DB1 generated 500MB of redo every fifteen minutes, and database DB4 generated 200MB of redo every fifteen minutes, you would allocated redo logs sized at around 700MB or so to accommodate these two databases.

One more thing to add. All of these recommendations and whatever choices you make need to be done under the guidance of specific SLA's. For example, if you want to ensure that your very busy database will lose no more than one minute worth of data, then log file switching every ten or fifteen minutes will never meet that requirement. As always, you need to pepper suggestions and best practices with the requirements of reality.

Before we leave the topic of sizing online redo logs, we should take a second to discuss the ability to configure the redo log block size. Oracle Database 12c provides the ability to define the redo block size. The default redo block size on most platforms is 512 bytes. There are now drives out there, such as solid state drives, that have block sizes that are higher than 512 bytes (4k seems to be the most common). You want to make sure that the redo log block size aligns with the block size of the disks that are being written too. Oracle supports block sizes of 512, 1024 and 4096 bytes. Some disks perform these 4k rights natively and some of them perform them in what is called emulation mode. If your disks are using 4k native mode then you must use a 4k redo log block size. If your disks are using 4k emulation mode, then Oracle recommends using 4k block sizes in that case too.

You can define the block size of a redo log when you create it by using the new **blocksize** parameter of the **alter database add log file** command. Here is an example:

```
Alter database add log file group 4 blocksize 4096;
```

If you try to change the block size to a value that is not the current disk sector size, Oracle will return an error such as the following:

```
Alter database add log file group 4 blocksize 4096
*
ERROR at line 1:
ORA-01378: The logical block size (4096) of file
C:\APP\ROBERT\ORADATA\ROBERTCDB\ONLINELOG\O1_MF_4_%U_.LOG
is not compatible with the disk sector size (media sector
size is 512 and host sector size is 512)
```

This message is telling you that your disks are not using 4096 byte sector size, and therefore you must be off your rocker because this setting will cause terrible things to happen to your performance. Ok, that's not exactly word for word what it's saying, but you get the point. If you are using emulation mode, you will need to set the hidden parameter **_disk_sector_size_override** to TRUE before you can define the block size bigger than 512 bytes.

If you are using ASM, you can also use 4k block sizes. However, there are some issues with the use of asmlib and you should check with Oracle before you use modified block sizes when asmlib is in use.

Note!

This same recommendation to use the larger block size with the online redo logs applies to setting of the DB_BLOCK_SIZE parameter of the database. If you are using 4k native mode disks, then your DB_BLOCK_SIZE of the database much be 4k or larger. Also, when creating disk groups you will need to create them using the sector_size attribute and setting the sector_size to 4k. ASM also has other rules related to using 4k sector sizes. Review the Oracle documentation and MOS for more information on this feature.

Now that we know how much redo log space we need for our existing database, we need to add space for any new databases where we have no real idea of the redo generation rate. Let's look at that next.

Sizing Redo for an Unknown Database

Trying to figure out the unknown is a tough job. When you have a database that someone is starting to develop, or that a outside vendor is going to provide and dump data into – you have no way to historically know how to size the redo logs for that database. It's enough to make you tear your hair out.

However, I can help you with some guidelines. First, usually any database is going to go through some testing. During testing, sizing of the online redo logs can be a totally wild guess. I would start with some value that approximates the amount of data changes you expect the database will go through every fifteen minutes. If you don't even know for sure what that would be, I'd opt to configure large log files rather than small ones, because small log files will have a significant impact on performance, while larger log files will have on space availability. The DBCA creates log files that are 52M in size. This is usually universally to small for any kind of production database that is going to have moderate volume.

Generally, I would start out with log files that are around 500MB in size. If you know the database is going to be hit hard by DML operations, log files 1GB or even larger are not unusual. Once you have created your log files, you can monitor how often they are switching, and monitor the redo log advisor to determine if you need to size them up or down. Also, there are certain database wait events that, if they are causing significant wait times, are usually dead give aways that your log files are too small. If you see significant waits for anything that say 'latch: redo *', you might have a problem with your redo logs being too small.

If you do need to adjust the sizing of your online redo logs, this can easily be done online. You can drop any inactive online redo log group, as long as it has been archived. Once you drop the online redo log group, then you can add the new (probably larger) online redo log group. These are pretty standard DBA operations and are no different in a CDB environment, so I'm not going to spend time showing you how to drop and re-create redo log files.

Once you have determined how much redo your unknown databases are likely to need, add that amount to the amount you calculated for the existing databases that you can at least get some reasonably reliable data for. This is going to be a good starting point at sizing your online redo logs then for your CDB. Generally, I recommend three groups with two members each to begin with. If your online redo log files are large enough, then three groups should be plenty.

Determining Memory Requirements for the CDB

Memory is a topic that I see DBA's just somehow go so wrong with when moving databases to new hardware, during upgrades and when moving to a Multitenant configuration. Usually what I see them do is just pick up a database, along with its SPFILE, and plop it down wherever it is supposed to go, and turn it on. Somehow they assume memory is properly configured to begin with. I have lost track of how many times I discovered that the memory on the old box was not configured correctly. More often than not, I find that memory is way over allocated, as opposed to under allocated – but I see a fair share of both.

The process of determining how much memory to configure a CDB with is similar to the process of determining the size of the online redo logs. For known databases, rather than looking just at the configuration of memory in the parameter file, you should also take a look at the output of the various memory advisors that Oracle makes available such as the V$MEMORY_TARGET_ADVICE or V$SGA_TARGET_ADVICE views (depending on how you have configured your memory). These advisors are also available from Oracle Cloud Control 12c. Take a moment to rationalize the amount of memory that you are currently using against the amount of memory the advisors recommend.

This advice extends beyond the SGA to the PGA as well. V$PGA_TARGET_ADVICE provides PGA sizing recommendations that you can use to determine how to best configure the PGA sizing parameter such as PGA_AGGREGATE_LIMIT and PGA_AGGREGATE_TARGET.

A CDB can use any of the available memory configuration options available in Oracle Database 12c. So you can use AMM, ASMM or manual memory management as you see fit. I'd mention the use of huge pages in Linux, but that always seems to start a holy war of sorts. I think that there are times to use HugePages and times not to use HugePages. My preference is not to use them unless you can clearly articulate the reasons you want to start using them on your current system (other than something like "someone told me so"). There is plenty of information on the good, bad and ugly related to HugePages, so I will leave that to your own research.

Other Options You Can Use To Properly Test and Configure Your CDB

I have you the standard command line ways that you can use to figure out how much space to allocate to your new CDB. There are also some other tools that can be incredibly handy. Some of them require a license and others just require they be configured.

Let's start with Oracle Real-Application Testing (RAT). In spite of an unfortunate acronym, RAT really is a first class testing tool. With RAT, you can configure your new CDB and make a copy of the production databases that you will eventually be consolidating over to the CDB. You can then record the workload that these databases do in production, and then you can replay that workload on the CDB. The really slick thing is that you can replay the workload for all of the PDB's in parallel, thus exercising the CDB as it really would be when all of the databases are running on it in production.

With RAT, you can get an early eye on things like memory allocations, redo log sizing and many other things that can go wrong if you don't properly test systems. If you are moving highly concurrent systems over to a CDB, it's even more important that you allow RAT to help you make sure that you won't run into any snags. The more concurrency any system experiences, the more things that can have problems. It's always best to get an early jump on any tuning or configuration modifications that you will need to do, before you go into actual production.

Oracle Cloud Control can easily lead you through the capture and replay of transactions using RAT. The Cloud Control repository will store the results for as long as you need them, and you can produce a number of reports that allow you to review any regression issues that might have occurred.

Oracle Enterprise Manager Cloud Control also provides a new tool called the Oracle Enterprise Manager 12c Consolidation Tool. This tool can help you investigate the impacts of consolidating from various environments onto a single environment. You can run various scenarios such as varying workloads between different databases, and being able to look at your consolidation planning from different perspectives. The Consolidation Tool also is aware of the various performance metrics of the hardware you will be moving from and the hardware you will be moving too and uses those metrics as a part of its capacity forecasting. We will cover OEM, including the Consolidation Tool in much more detail in Book Three of this series.

Determining the Character Set of the CDB

We have mentioned the importance of choosing the correct character set already. Character sets can be one of the biggest got ya's there is when it comes to databases. In Oracle Database 12c Release 1 all of the PDB's must have the same character set as the CDB. Oracle recommends that you use the Unicode character set (AL32UTF8) whenever possible for a new CDB.

If you have databases that have other character sets, you will need to export them and then import them into a pre-created PDB. It is beyond the scope of this book to talk about all of the considerations that go with moving a database with one character set to a database with another character set. Oracle provides a manual called the Database Globalization Support Guide to assist you in efforts that involve changing character sets.

Oracle Database 12c includes a new tool to assist you in database character set migrations to Unicode. The Database Migration Assistant for Unicode (DMU) provides a guided workflow that helps you in your effort to migrate to a Unicode character set. Obviously, you will need to make sure that your application will work with a different character set, but moving to Unicode is something to consider. One note about DMU. It currently does not support PDB's. Therefore, if you want to use it for character set conversions you will need to convert a non-Multitenant database. If you have a PDB that you want to convert, you can unplug it from the CDB and convert it into a non-Multitenant database. Once that has been completed, you can execute the character migration with DMU. Once the character migration is complete, you can plug the database back into the CDB.

Obviously, if you want to migrate the character set of a non-Multitenant database that you also want to plug into a CDB, you should perform the character set migration first. Once that is complete, then you can plug it into the CDB.

If you have databases that have different character sets that cannot be converted, then you can simply create a CDB to contain those databases. Many CDB's can run on the same server, just like many non-Multitenant databases can run on the same server.

If you want to use DMU, make sure you download the most current version first.

Other Parameters that Deserve Consideration when Creating a CDB

When you create a PDB it will inherit the parameter settings/configuration of the parent CDB. While there are a few changes that can be made at the PDB level, they are very few and in general there isn't a lot of granularity in configuration at the instance level. SO, when you are preparing to create a CDB, there are some database parameters that you will want to make sure are set properly. Because there is just one instance and one instance parameter file, all of the parameters in the parameter file will impact every PDB. There are some system parameters that can be set specific to a PDB. We will cover these in more detail in Chapter 4.

The following parameters should be reviewed when you are creating your CDB:

- The PROCESSES parameter – If you plan to run more than one PDB, it makes sense that there may be a requirement to support additional processes. Consider too that the PDB's themselves may use Oracle features that require additional processed, such as Advanced Queuing or the Job Scheduler. Also consider that there will be additional users connecting to the instance and each of those connections will require a process.

- Memory related parameters – MEMORY_TARGET, SGA_TARGET, PGA_AGGREGATE_TARGET, PGA_AGGREGATE_LIMIT and more.

- DB_BLOCK_SIZE – Remember, the block size will be shared by all of the PDB's in that database. If you are going to plug-in a non-Multitenant database, making it a PDB, then that database needs to have the same block size as the CDB. If you have databases with different block sizes, you may want to create two different CDB's to accommodate the different block sizes required.

There are some ways to work around the block size issue. You can create a tablespace with the block size of the CDB. You can then configure memory areas in the SGA for non-standard block sizes. Then you would use transportable tablespaces and transport in the tablespaces with the non-default block sizes. At this point, best practice would be to move the objects in the tablespace with the non-standard block size into new tablespaces that are the standard block size of the CDB.

Two other obvious solutions are to use Data Pump to move the data into the new PDB or you can use a database link and suck up the data using a CTAS or similar command.

- PDB_FILE_NAME_CONVERT – This parameter is used to define naming conversions that should take place during the creation of a PDB from the SEED database. You should not normally need to use this parameter.

  It is strongly recommended (not just by Oracle but by yours truly) that you enable and use Oracle Managed Files from the beginning of the creation of the CDB.

- DB_CREATE_FILE_DEST – Defines the base of the default location that the Oracle Database will start creating directories and OMF related files.

- DB_CREATE_ONLINE_LOG_DEST_n – Defines the default location (or ASM disk group) for redo logs file and control files to be created. This parameter can have 5 different iterations within the database parameter file of a database. Iterations are distinguished by a unique number (1 to 5) represented by the n

placeholder in the parameter name here. This allows for automated multiplexing of online redo logs and control files.

Know What's Not Supported

Oracle defines what is not supported in a Multitenant database in the readme file for the Oracle Database. As of the writing of this book, Oracle Database 12.1.0.2 has been released and the following Oracle features are not supported in a CDB database:

- Flashback Transaction Query
- Flashback Transaction Backout
- Database Change Notification
- Continuous Query Notification
- Client Side Cache
- Heat map
- Automatic Data Optimization
- Oracle Streams
- Oracle Fail Safe release 4.1.0 that ships with Oracle Database 12.1.0.2. Oracle Fail Safe 4.1.1.0 will support the Oracle CDB/PDB architecture

If you are going to need to use any of these features in your database, then it cannot be contained within a CDB.

Note!

Do keep in mind that it's very possible that any future release of 12c (including . (dot) releases) will add any of these functions into the CDB architecture. So, don't discount using CDB's until you have checked the latest documentation. I'm going to try to keep this book up to date as much as possible but you never know!

We have now covered the pre-requisites specific to the creation of a CDB database. Keep in mind that this list did not contain the additional requirements that are associated with the creation of all Oracle databases, so you will need to make sure you meet those needs as well. Also, keep in mind that with each new release of Oracle Database there may be new, modified or dropped requirements. So, use this book as your guide, but always check and make sure that something else isn't going to stand in your way to Multitenant happiness.

CDB Database Creation

Time to make the doughnuts, or in our case, create our CDB database. Keep in mind, all we are doing right now is creating the CDB, although the DBCA will create a PDB for us. After the CDB is created, then we would start creating or plugging in PDB's.

CDB database creation is almost the same as creating a non-Multitenant database. In this chapter, we are going to assume that you are familiar with the creation of non-Multitenant databases. Therefore we will just hit the "highlights" involved in the creation of the database. We will discuss creating a CDB both manually and with the DBCA. So, let's get to it!

Creating a CDB Manually

Creating a CDB manually is almost the same as creating a non-Multitenant database. You use the same **create database statement** along with the same parameters. There are some new parameters that are used, and I want to focus on those. First, let's look at a **create database** statement that will result in the creation of a CDB database:

```
-- assuming the use of omf
-- assume directories needed have already been created
-- db_create_file_dest='/u01/app/oracle/oradata'
-- db_create_online_log_dest_1='/u01/app/oracle/oradata'
-- must create controlfile, redolog and datafile
directories.
create database rfcdba
user sys identified by crackup
user system identified by crackerjack
log file group 1 size 200m blocksize 512,
        group 2 size 200m blocksize 512,
        group 3 size 200m blocksize 512
maxloghistory 1 maxlog files 16
maxlogmembers 3 maxdatafiles 1024
character set al32utf8
national character set al16utf16
extent management local
datafile size 1000m autoextend on next 100m maxsize
unlimited
```

```
sysaux datafile size 550m autoextend on next 100m maxsize
unlimited default tablespace deftbs
datafile size 500m autoextend on
next 100m maxsize unlimited
default temporary tablespace tempts1
tempfile size 100m autoextend on next 10m
maxsize unlimited
undo tablespace undotbs1
datafile size 200m autoextend on next 5m
maxsize unlimited
enable pluggable database
seed
system datafiles size 300m autoextend on
next 50m maxsize unlimited
sysaux datafiles size 100m;
```

So, let's look at what is different about this create database statement with respect to Multitenant databases. Probably the most obvious thing is the **enable pluggable database** statement, which is part of the new **enable_pluggable_database** clause of the **create database** statement. This is the key to the creation of a CDB. Unless a database is created using this clause, then it is not a CDB. Remember, you cannot convert an existing Multitenant database into a CDB. You can, however, move an existing non-Multitenant database into a CDB as a PDB.

The next thing to notice is the definition of the SEED container as seen here:

```
SEED
SYSTEM DATAFILES SIZE 125M AUTOEXTEND ON NEXT 10M MAXSIZE
UNLIMITED
SYSAUX DATAFILES SIZE 100M
```

Here, the characteristics of the SEED container are defined. There are two main tablespaces in the SEED container being defined here: SYSTEM and SYSAUX. Each of these tablespaces have their datafile attributes defined in this clause. Since these tablespace are created in the SEED container, they will subsequently be created in any PDB that is created, using the SEED container as the source container. The same sizes and datafile configurations will be used in the cloned databases.

> **Note!**
>
> The DBCA provides a really good way to see how to properly create any Oracle database. If you define the database attributes in the DBCA and then, instead of creating a database, you would simply choose for it to create the files required to manually create the database. You can then review these files and modify them for your specific purposes. This method ensures that you run all the scripts and fulfill the other requirements to create the database with the feature set you desire.

Once the **create database** command has completed executing, you will have created a basic CDB. It will consist of the main CDB called RFCDB. That CDB will have its own SYSTEM, SYSAUX, UNDO and default temporary tablespaces defined. It will also have the SEED container within it as we already discussed. The CDB will be opened in READ WRITE mode, while the SEED container will be in READ ONLY mode, which is the mode it belongs in.

After the **create database** command is complete, there are other scripts to be executed when creating a CDB database, just as there is in a non-Multitenant database. In the case of a CDB you will run the script $ORACLE_HOME/rdbms/admin/catcdb.sql from the **sys as sysdba** account of the CDB. Depending on what options you are running in the database, you may need to run other scripts. Check the documentation for the options you are running for more information on any other post-database creation steps.

Other things you will probably want to do, that you would do with a non-Multitenant database are create a password file, backup the database and enable the automated startup of the database when the server starts. You may also want to configure EM Express manually, which is no different between a CDB and non-CDB database.

Once the rfcdba CDB is created, you will end up with an Oracle Multitenant database that looks like the one shown in figure 2-2. In this figure you have your CDB (called CDB$ROOT) with one container, the SEED container (called PDB$SEED), attached to it. At this point, we are ready to start creating PDB's.

Warning!

When this book was written there were some bugs with respect to manually creating an Oracle CDB database. Oracle recommends that you use the DBCA to avoid these errors. MOS Document 1948487.1 discusses this issue in more detail.

Figure 2-2 An Oracle CDB After Its Creation by the DBCA

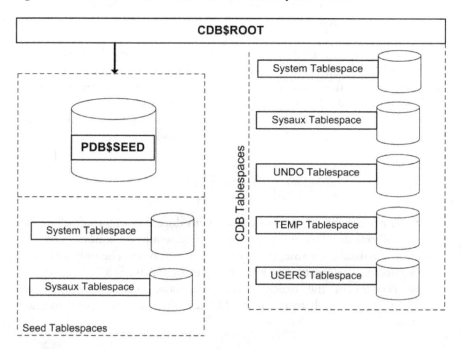

Creating a CDB using the DBCA

I will say at the outset here, using the DBCA is my preferred method to create databases. There are a number of reasons for this. I think though that one of the main reasons is that the process to create a database manually can change as time goes on. While it's good to keep up with these changes, the fact of the matter is that DBCA always keeps up with all of the changes. DBCA adheres to a set of standards defined by Oracle. Additionally DBCA takes care of all of the annoying details for you, like creating a password file or making network related entries.

If your enterprise uses DBCA and its templates, then it will be easier for the organization to define, implement and enforce those standards. The DBCA provides one standardized way of doing things, and this is a good thing. You will also see in the next section that the DBCA provides a nice standardized way to manage the creation, removal, plug-in and unplug of PDB's into the CDB. There are a number of reasons to use the DBCA, and I'm not going to spend a lot of time here listing them – but it's a very important tool, and you should use it if at all possible.

Creating a CDB with the DBCA is almost exactly like creating a non-CDB with the DBCA. Because of this, I am only going to highlight the specific differences and perhaps point out a thing or two. So, not a lot of pictures of screen output here!

After starting the DBCA you will choose the create database option, which will bring up the create database dialogue. It is this next screen (creation mode) that you will treat differently since you are creating a Multitenant capable database. There are two options you can choose from here. You can choose the option "Create a database with default configuration" or you can choose "Advanced Mode".

Creating a Database Using the Default Configuration Option of DBCA

If you choose the "Create a database with default configuration" option, you will fill out the dialogue boxes just as you would for a non-CDB. You will choose a database name, storage options and so on. The only difference with respect to the creation of a CDB capable database is a little check box at the bottom of the dialogue box that says, "Create As Container Database". If you wish to create a CDB database then you need to check that box.

Below that checkbox is a dialogue box that is titled, "Pluggable Database Name". When you create a CDB from the DBCA, it will create a single PDB, that you have named in the dialogue box on this page, at the same time. This is not optional, however, after the CDB is created you can easily drop that PDB if you need too. Once you click on the Next button you will proceed through the remainder of the dialogue boxes in the same way you would with a non-CDB. When the final dialogue box appears, you will simply click the "Finish" button and start the creation of your CDB. Figure 2-3 provides a screen print of the create database page, showing the two options that are available, as well as where to define that the database is a container database if you are using the default configuration mode.

Figure 2-3 DBCA Create a Database with Default Configuration Option Page

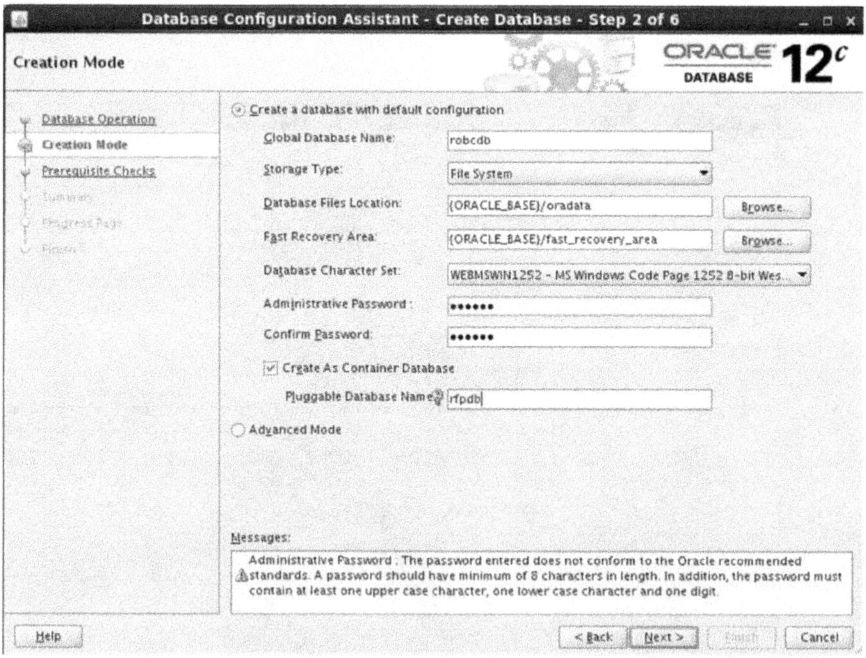

Creating a Database Using the Advanced Mode Configuration Option of DBCA

If you choose "Advanced Mode" from the first create database dialogue page, you will click on Next and be taken to the database template page. You should be familiar with this page already. Any of the templates you choose will be able to support the creation of a CDB. Choose your template and click on next.

The next page will be the Database Identification page that you will indicate that the database to be created is to be created as a container database. This page provides the ability for you to create 0,1 or more PDB's at the time the CDB is created. If you choose to create more than 1 container database, the name of the container databases that are created will be prefixed by the name you choose on this dialogue page. Oracle will attach a unique identifier to the end of the PDB name. This eliminates the risk of namespace collisions within the CDB. DBCA can create up to 252 PDBs for you this way, which happens to be the maximum number of

PDBs allowed in a single CDB. Figure 2-4 provides a screen print of the Database Identification screen that you will see when following the Advance Mode workflow:

Figure 2-4 DBCA Advanced Mode Database Identification Configuration Page

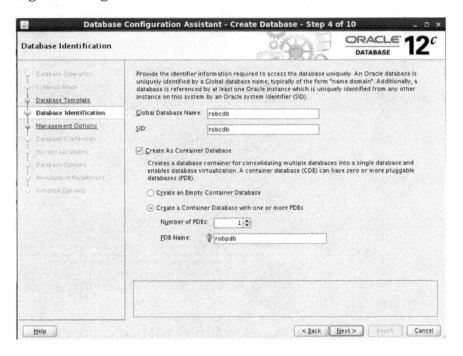

Once you have indicated that you want to create the database as a CDB, the rest of the flow is the same as a regular non-CDB database. You may want to review the initialization parameters when the initialization parameters box appears, just to make sure that they are configured correctly for your database. It is also on this screen that you can change the character set that you want to use. Again, you might want to review the character set setting to make sure it meets your needs.

The Initialization Parameters page also provides the location where you will define how memory will be assigned to the CDB. We discussed a number of considerations when it comes to memory earlier in this chapter and you will want to apply what you know to the decisions involving memory allocations. Further this page also provides the ability to define the number of processes (in the sizing tab) that you want to configure the database for. Again, we discussed the importance of properly sizing the processes value. Figure 2-5 provides a look at the Initialization Parameters page with the memory tab selected. You can see that there are also tabs for Sizing and Character Sets, which you will want to review. Finally, at the bottom of the page, you will see a button called "All Initialization Parameters". You may want to click on that button to review the database parameters and ensure they are configured as you desire.

Figure 2-5 DBCA Advanced Mode Initialization Parameters Page

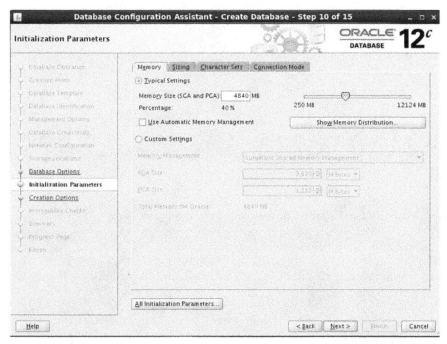

The rest of the DBCA database creation workflow is the same as with a non-CDB database. When the DBCA has completed the database creation you will have a CDB that is capable of hosting one or more PDB's.

Connecting to the CDB

Connecting to a CDB is no different than connecting to an Oracle Non-Multitenant database. You simply set your environment so that the ORACLE_SID variable (or its equivalent) is set to the name of the CDB. Obviously any other environment variables such as the PATH, need to be set correctly as well. Once that is done, you just use SQL*Plus and log into the CDB. In this example, we have configured our environment, logged into the CDB and queried the V$DATABASE columns NAME and CDB. NAME is the name of the database, of course. The CDB column indicates if the database is, or is not, a container database. Here is the example:

```
C:\orion>set ORACLE_SID=robertcdb
C:\orion>sqlplus / as sysdba
SQL*Plus: Release 12.1.0.2.0 Production on Sat Jan 10
18:59:25 2015
Copyright (c) 1982, 2014, Oracle.  All rights reserved.
Connected to:
Oracle Database 12c Enterprise Edition Release 12.1.0.2.0 -
64bit Production
With the Partitioning, OLAP, Advanced Analytics and Real
Application Testing options

SQL> select name, cdb from v$database;

NAME       CDB
---------  ---
ROBERTCD   YES
```

You can also connect to the CDB through a network connection by making a SQL*Plus call to the CDB's service name as seen here:

```
Sqlplus sys/password@mycdb
```

You can also use the easy connect format as seen here:

```
Sqlplus sys/password@//serverone:1525/mycdb
```

Connecting to a PDB is a bit different, and we will discuss that in the next chapter.

Summary

In this chapter I walked you through the steps you will follow when creating a Container Database. We talked about a lot of the pre-requisite tasks that you need to complete (or think about) first, and then we discussed creating the CDB. We covered creating a CDB manually first, and then we continued with a discussion on creating a CDB with the DBCA. In the next section we will discuss creating a PDB within a CDB.

3
CREATING AND REMOVING PDBS

Now that you have created a Container Database the next step is to create a PDB within that container database. In this section we will discuss the creation and removal of PDBS. We will look at how to manually create a PDB, and also we will look at using the DBCA to create PDBS. After that, we will show you how you connect to PDB's using their service name. Finally we will cover removing PDB's either through the use of the **drop pluggable database** command or by using the DBCA.

Connecting to a PDB

Connecting to a PDB is somewhat different than connecting to a non-Multitenant database or a CDB. With a non-Multitenant database or a CDB you will set the database environment such as ORACLE_SID to the SIR of the database and then connect to it via SQL*Plus.

With a PDB there is no environment variable that you can use to connect to a PDB. Instead, you must indicate the service name of the PDB to connect too. You can do this using the familiar @ connection method with SQL*Plus as seen here:

```
sqlplus myuser/password@mypdb
```

This means that to be able to connect to the PDB that the PDB must be open and the database listener must be running and the PDB service must be registered with the listener. You can also use the EZNaming syntax which includes the host name, the listener port servicing the PDB and the service name of the PDB. Here is an example of using the EXNaming syntax:

```
Sqlplus myuser/password@//myhost:1522/mypdb
```

Creating a PDB Manually

Now that we have gotten our CDB created, it's time to do the real work – create the PDBs we want to use. That is what this section is all about. There are several ways to create a new PDB. In this chapter we will concentrate on the use of the **create pluggable database** command which is used to manually create databases. The **create pluggable database** command can be used to create PDB's in a number of ways including

- Creating a PDB using the SEED container
- Creating a PDB by cloning an existing PDB with or without data
- Creating a PDB by cloning an existing PDB Over a database link

Let's take a look at these methods next.

Creating a PDB Using the Seed Container

The first way the **create pluggable database** command can be used to create a PDB is to have it use the SEED container. We have mentioned the SEED container before. It is, essentially, a wholly self-contained PDB that is reserved for the creation of other PDB's. It contains its own SYSTEM and SYSAUX tablespaces. It may also contain its own default user tablespace. The design of the SEED container enables the really fast creation of new PDBs within the CDB.

The command itself is pretty straight forward. You will need to indicate the name and password of the administrative user. To create a PDB from the SEED container you need to login to the CDB as an administrative user using the SYSDBA privilege. This might be SYS or a common user (which we will discuss in chapter 5). Once you are logged in then you would issue the **create pluggable database** command as seen here:

```
Create pluggable database newpdb admin user newadmin
identified by password roles=(dba);
```

This will create a new pluggable database called NEWPDB. This will also create an administrative user in the PDB called NEWADMIN. Note that we used the roles keyword to assign the DBA role to the admin user. By default, when the admin user is created it's granted only one privilege and one role called PDB_DBA. The default privileges that the admin account are granted are:

- **Unlimited tablespace**
- **Create pluggable database** (through a grant to the PDB_DBA role)
- **Create session** (through a grant to the PDB_DBA role)
- **Set container** (through a grant to the PDB_DBA role)

A PDB admin user also does not have SYSDBA privileges and cannot be granted SYSDBA privileges. Thus, the scope of the admin user is restricted to the PDB only. Once the PDB has been created, you can see it in the V$PDBS view as seen here:

```
SQL> select name, open_mode from v$pdbs;

NAME                                OPEN_MODE
---------------------------------   ----------
PDB$SEED                            READ ONLY
NEWPDB                              MOUNTED
```

Notice that the OPEN_MODE of the NEWPDB PDB is MOUNTED. The **create pluggable database** command does not open the PDB once it's been created. This is done by the DBA using the **alter pluggable database open** command as seen here:

```
SQL> alter pluggable database newpdb open;
Pluggable database altered.
```

Now we can see that the OPEN_MODE has changed:

```
SQL> select name, open_mode from v$pdbs;

NAME                                OPEN_MODE
---------------------------------   ----------
PDB$SEED                            READ ONLY
ROBERTPDB                           MOUNTED
TPLUG                               READ WRITE
NEWPDB                              READ WRITE
```

There are a number of options your might choose from when creating a PDB. First, if you are not using OMF, then you will need to use the **file_name_convert** clause to indicate where the files of the new PDB should be located. For example, if the SEED container datafiles are in a directory called /u01/app/oracle/oradata/mycdb/datafile. You want to create a new PDB called NEWPDB in the directory /u01/app/oracle/oradata/mycdb/newpdb/datafile, and you are not using OMF. You will need to indicate the directory path conversion that you wish to use by using the **file_name_convert** clause. Here is an example:

```
Create pluggable database newpdb admin user newpdb
identified by password
file_name_convert=
('/u01/app/oracle/oradata/mycdb/datafile',
'/u01/app/oracle/oradata/mycdb/newpdb');
```

Note that the **file_name_convert** option is not available if you are using OMF.

You can also include the **pdb_storage_clause** to control the amount of physical storage that the PDB can consume on the server. You can control the total size of the PDB or you can control how much space it will consume if it's using a shared temporary tablespace in the database. The default is no limits are placed on the PDB when it is created.

Creating a PDB Cloning an Existing Local PDB with or Without Data

The **create pluggable database** command can also be used to create a new PDB from an existing PDB. You use the **create pluggable database** to do this along with the **create_pdb_clone** clause is used to make a clone of a PDB. To clone a PDB the source PDB needs to be open and then you issue the **create pluggable database** command as seen here where we are creating a PDB called COPYPDB from a PDB called MYPDB:

```
-- open the PDB
Alter pluggable database mypdb open;
Create pluggable database copypdb from mypdb;
```

This will create the PDB along with the network services needed to access it. The data from the MYPDB will be copied in this case, so we will end up with an exact copy of the MYPDB PDB.

Often what we would like to do is just clone the database and all of the data structures within it, but not copy the data in the user tablespaces. You can use the **no data** option of the **create pluggable database** command to do that as seen in this example:

```
Alter pluggable database mypdb open;
Create pluggable database copypdb from mypdb no data;
```

Note that using the **no data** option can only be done if you are copying data between PDB's. If you are creating a PDB from a non-CDB database then a no data copy is not available. Additionally the following restrictions apply when using the **nodata** clause:

- The PDB cannot contain clustered tables in user schemas
- The PDB cannot contain Advanced Queuing tables
- Index-organized tables
- Tables that contain abstract data type columns

Cloning a PDB From a PDB over a Network Link

In this section we will discuss the creation of a new PDB based on a PDB in another CDB over a network link. First, we will address the requirements to create a remote PDB and then we will discuss how to configure the databases for the cloning. Then we will discuss how to do the cloning itself.

Preparing to Clone a PDB over a Network Link

Before you can clone a PDB, you must meet certain requirements that include:

- Both the source and destination CDBs are open and are not in read-only, upgrade or downgrade mode.
- Decide the name of the new PDB to be created should be unique on the server and/or cluster to avoid naming collisions.
- The source and destination platforms must have the same endianness
- The source and destination CDB's must have the same database options installed.
- The source and destination CDB's must be the same character set.

If these requirements are met, then you must to the following to prepare to clone the PDB. I will cover this in the next section.

Cloning a PDB over a Network Link

Now that you have completed all the prerequisites related to the cloning of a remote PDB you are now ready to perform the cloning. Here are the steps of that cloning:

1. Connect to the source CDB and shutdown the source PDB.
2. Startup the source CDB in read only mode.
3. Connect to the target CDB.
4. Issue the **create pluggable database** command and clone the database.
5. Shutdown the cloned PDB and then open it for read write activity.
6. Shutdown the source PDB and open it for read write activity.

In our example the source CDB is called srccdb and the source PDB is called srcpdb. The target CDB is called targcdb and the target PDB is called targpdb.

1. Log into the source CDB as SYS and change to the PDB that you
    will be cloning using the **alter session set container** command.

```
set ORACLE_SID=srecdb
sqlplus / as sysdba
alter session set container=srcpdb;
```

2. In the source PDB, create a user in the PDB or decide what user
    you want to use to connect to facilitate the cloning. Grant that
    user the **create session** and **create pluggable database**
    privileges if they do not already have those privileges.

```
Create user copy_user identified by copy_user;
Grant create session, create pluggable database to
copy_user;
```

3. Put the source PDB in read-only mode.

```
set ORACLE_SID=srecdb
sqlplus / as sysdba
Alter pluggable database srcpdb close;
Alter pluggable database srcpdb open read only;
```

4. In the target CDB, log in as the SYS user.

```
set ORACLE_SID=targcdb
sqlplus / as sysdba
```

5. Create a database link that connects to the service name of the
    source PDB.

```
Create database link copy_link
connect to copy_user identified by copy_user
Using '//myserver:1521/srcpdb';
```

6. You are now ready to clone the database. Use the **create
    pluggable database** command using the from option to clone
    over the network as seen here:

```
Create pluggable database targpdb from
copy_user@copy_link;
```

7. Once the new PDB has been created it will be open in READ
    ONLY mode. Check the status of the new PDB and then use the

alter pluggable database command to close the new PDB and then re-open it.

```
set ORACLE_SID=targcdb
sqlplus / as sysdba
select name, open_mode from v$pdbs;
Alter pluggable database targpdb close;
Alter pluggable database targpdb open;
select name, open_mode from v$pdbs;
```

8. You can now take the source PDB and shut it down and re-open it.

```
set ORACLE_SID=srecdb
sqlplus / as sysdba
Alter pluggable database srcpdb close;
Alter pluggable database srcpdb open read only;
```

If you now check the V$PDBS view on the target database you will see the new PDB has been created and that it is open:

```
SQL> select name from v$pdbs;

NAME
------------------------------
PDB$SEED
ROBERTPDB
TPLUG
TARGPDB
```

Note!

I will discuss unplugging and plugging in CDB's in Book 2 of this series.

Creating a PDB Via the DBCA

You can use the DBCA to create PDB's. With the DBCA you can create a pluggable database from the SEED CDB. The DBCA can also be used to plug in and unplug PDB's which we will discuss in chapter 7. Let's look at how to create a pluggable database via DBCA.

Creating a PDB with the DBCA from the Seed Database

To create a PDB with the DBCA you need to first start the DBCA interface. Once you do, the DBCA Welcome Screen will appear which will provide you with an option titled "Manage Pluggable Databases" as seen in Figure 3-1. Select that option and click on Next to get to the next option.

Figure 3-1 DBCA Welcome Screen

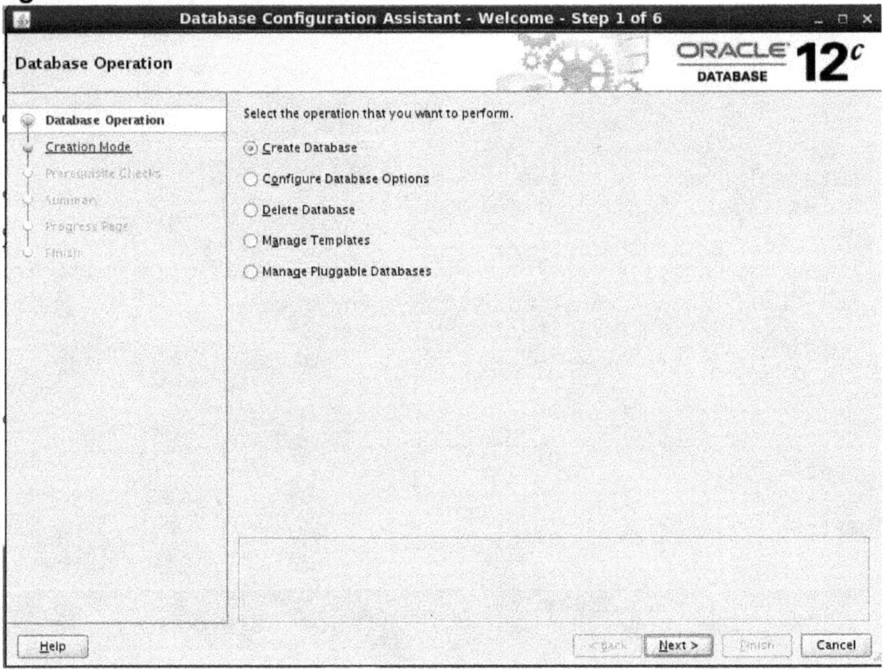

The next option, which you will see in Figure 3-2 is the "Manage Pluggable Databases" screen. Here you have several options. We are interested in the "Create Pluggable Database" option. It should already be selected. Ensure it is and then click on the Next button.

Figure 3-2 DBCA Manage Pluggable Databases Screen

In figure 3-3 we see the next DBCA screen which is titled "Database List". Here you will see a list of all of the CDB databases that are available on your system. Select the database that you want to create the PDB in. Next, you will need to put in administrative credentials for the CDB that you are going to create the PDB in. Once you have completed this work, click on the Next button.

Figure 3-3 DBCA Database List Screen

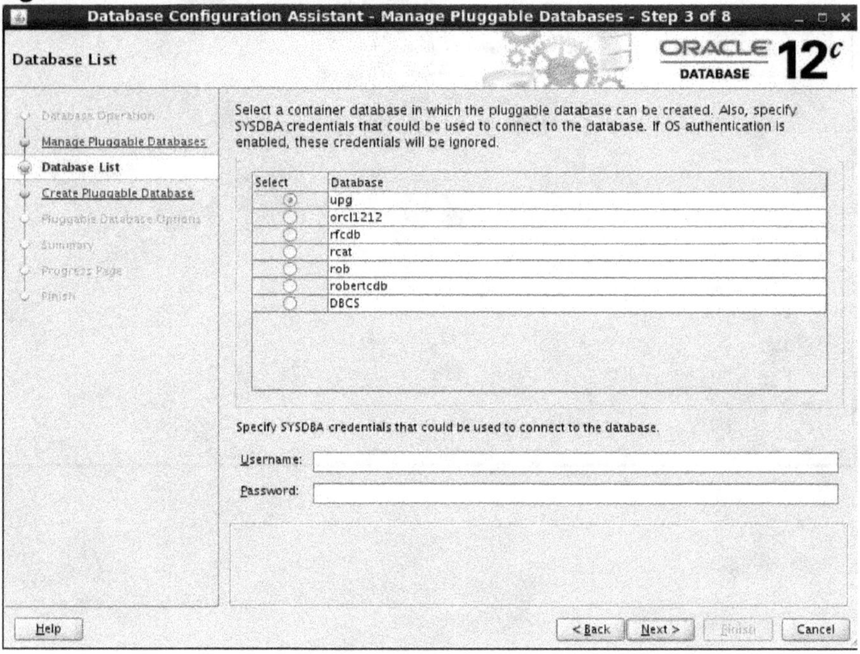

Having selected the database that you want to create the PDB in, the DBCA will take you to the "Create Pluggable Database" screen as seen in figure 3-4. Here you have an option to create a new pluggable database along with two other options. The other two options are used for plugging in databases and we will cover that functionality in Part Two of this book. Select the "Create a new Pluggable Database" option and click on Next to continue the creation of the pluggable database.

Figure 3-4 DBCA Create Pluggable Database Screen

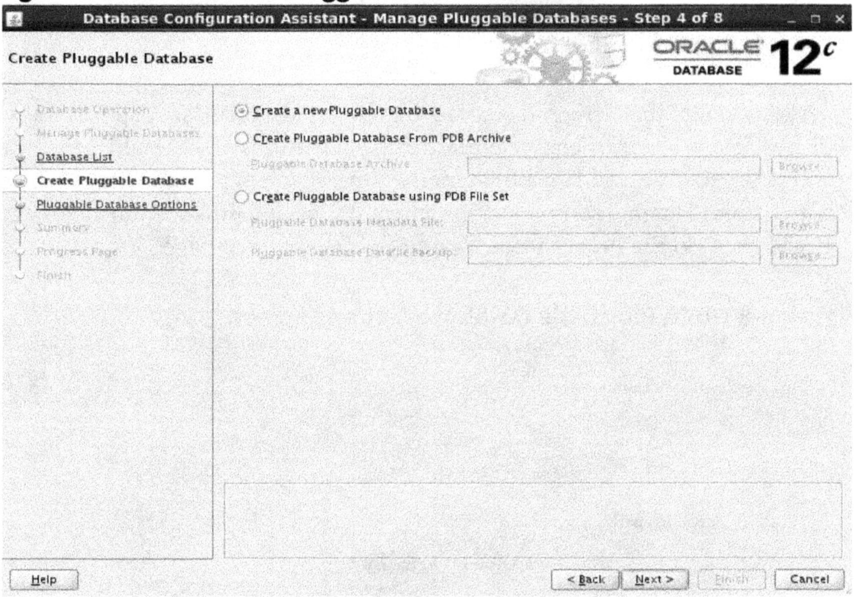

Figure 3-5, "Pluggable Database Options" is next. On this screen you will name our new pluggable database, which we called CREPDB in our example. Also you will be able to indicate if you want to use OMF or define a common location for the datafiles. I recommend that you use OMF. Additionally on this screen there is a checkbox to indicate if you want the DBCA to create a default user tablespace for you. You are not given an opportunity to name this tablespace though. When the PDB is created this tablespace will be called USERS. You will have the opportunity to change the name of this tablespace before you complete the PDB creation. The screen also has you indicate the administrator name and password for the new PDB that is being created.

Additionally, this screen has a tab that is listed Database Vault & Label Security. If you want to enable either of these features you should go to the tab and do so. We will not be changing any of the settings on that tab in this example. Having completed the entry of the information on this page you will click on the Next button again to go to the next page.

Figure 3-5 DBCA Pluggable Database Options Screen

Next, as seen in Figure 3-6 you will see the "Summary" page of the DBCA. A summary of all of the information you entered is presented. You should review all of this information to make sure it's correct.

Figure 3-6 DBCA Summary Screen

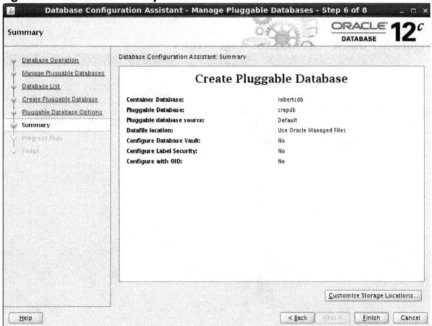

On the DBCA Summary page there is a button at the bottom called "Customize Storage Locations". If you click on this option you will see the Customize Storage page seen in Figure 3-7. On this page you will see a list of the objects that will be used and created during the PDB creation. The PDB Source Files indicates the source files in the SEED container that will be used to create this PDB.

Figure 3-7 DBCA Customize Storage Screen

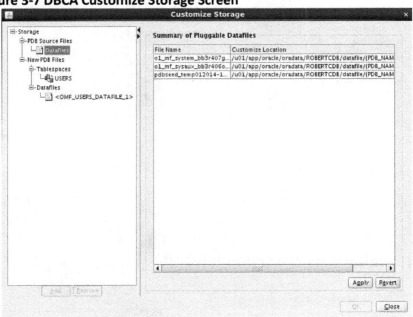

If you indicated earlier that you would like a default user data tablespace created, you can change the name of that tablespace in the Customize Storage Screen. There are a number of options you can take advantage of on this screen including changing the datafile name and size of the tablespace before it is created. You can add a datafile to the tablespace and you can define attributes of existing datafiles such as autoextend and the like. One thing you might consider on the Customize Storage Screen is to change the increment setting for each datafile with respect to autoextend. The default (1280k) is probably way to small for reality and can cause performance problems. At a minimum I recommend 64m extensions of datafiles. If you expect frequent extensions then I would make the increment size equivalent to 5 to 10 percent of the number of extensions that you would expect in a year. Round this value up to a multiple of 8 to allow for alignment with the database block size. For example, if our datafile is 1GB in size and you expect overall growth of 500MB over a year, you should probably set your increment to 64M (10% would be 56MB and we are rounding up to a multiple of 8). This will help to eliminate the performance impacts of large data file expansions during large data loads.

Returning to the Summary storage screen after making any storage modifications you can click on Finish. Once you do the DBCA will bring up the "Progress" page and begin the creation of the PDB. The progress page can be seen in Figure 3-7. Note that there is a progress bar at the top of the page that will indicate how far along the creation process you are in. The steps are listed in the middle of the screen.

During the PDB creation the DBCA provides you with two options to monitor the progress of the creation of the database. A click box for the Activity log associated with the creation of the PDB, and one for the Alert log of the CDB is available. When you click on either of these, then the related logging screen will appear. These screens are also seen in Figure 3-8.

Figure 3-8 DBCA Progress Page

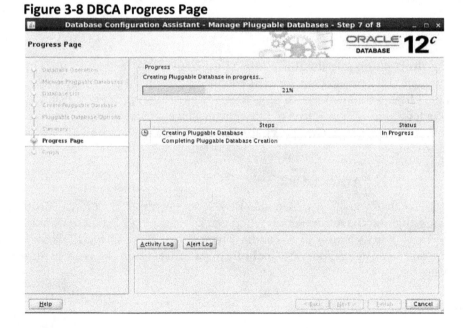

How long it takes for the PDB to be created is dependent on the speed of your database server, the underlying storage and other performance related issues. However, as you saw earlier, cloning a PDB from the SEED database does not take very long. When the cloning is completed the DBCA will indicate that it has completed the PDB creation with the message Pluggable database "name" plugged successfully" at which time you can click on the Close button and exit the DBCA.

The PDB that is created will be open in READ ONLY mode initially. You will want to open the PDB in READ WRITE mode, so that users can access it. To do this, log into the CDB and use the **alter pluggable database <PDB_NAME> close** command followed by the **alter pluggable database <PDB_NAME> open read write** command.

Dropping a PDB

Now that you know how to create PDB's, it's time to learn how to drop them. This can be done manually with the **drop pluggable database** or through the DBCA. We will discuss each of these options in the next section.

Dropping a PDB manually

The **drop pluggable database** is used to drop a PDB from a CDB. The command is pretty straight forward command. You need to be logged into the CDB as an administrative user, using the SYSDBA privilege. Once you have logged in, you will need to close the instance you are going to remove. This is done with the **alter pluggable database close** command as seen in this example:

```
Alter pluggable database tlug close;
```

Now that you have closed the PDB you can drop it with the **drop pluggable database** command. When you are dropping a database without unplugging (which we will discuss in Chapter 7 in Book 2) the PDB then you will need to include the **including datafiles** clause as seen in this example:

```
Drop pluggable database tlug including datafiles;
```

Dropping a PDB with DBCA

You can drop a PDB by using the DBCA. After starting the DBCA, you will see the DBCA Welcome Screen which will provide you with an option titled "Manage Pluggable Databases" as seen earlier in Figure 3-1. Select that "Manage Pluggable Databases" option and click on Next to get to the next option.

The next screen is you see will be the "Manage Pluggable Databases", which you can see in Figure 3-2 earlier in this section. Here you have several options. This time we are interested in the "Delete a Pluggable Database" option. It should already be selected. Ensure it is and then click on the Next button.

You will now be on the "Database List" screen that is shown in Figure 3-3 earlier in this section. From this screen you will choose the CDB that contains the PDB to be removed. Once you have selected the CDB, click on the Next button to continue.

Next you will see the Delete Pluggable Database screen as seen in Figure 3-9. This screen provides a drop down list of PDB's that are available to be dropped. Once you have selected the database to be removed, click on the Next button. This will lead to the DBCA Summary screen. This screen provides an over view of the activities to be performed. Click on Finish and the PDB will be deleted.

Figure 3-9 DBCA Delete Pluggable Database Page

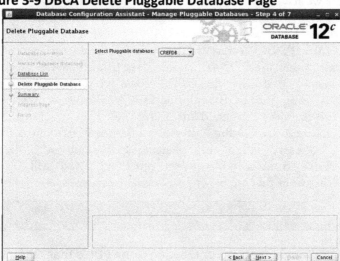

Renaming a PDB

PDB's can be renamed from the SQL prompt. This functionality does not exist in the DBCA. This is done through the **alter pluggable database** command, and including the **rename global_name** option. To rename the

PDB you have to be connected to the PDB through the **alter session set container** command. You would then open the PDB in restricted session mode using the **startup open restrict** command.

Once the PDB is open, issue the **alter pluggable database** command to rename the PDB. Oracle will also adjust the service name of the PDB to the name it is being changed to. Once the PDB is renamed you will take it out of restricted session and then it is ready to be used.

Here is an example of renaming a PDB called oldpdb to newpdb:

```
Sqlplus / as sysdba
Alter session set container=oldpdb;
Shutdown
Startup open restrict
Alter pluggable database oldpdb rename global_name to
newpdb;
Alter system disable restricted session;
```

Summary

In this chapter we have covered a large variety of ways that PDB's can be created in a CDB. We discussed creating PDB's by using the SEED container. We also discussed how to clone a PDB using another PDB as the source of the new PDB. We discussed how you can do this and either include the data within the PDB or without data from the PDB. We also discussed creating PDB's using the DBCA. Then we discussed dropping the PDB both using the PDB and the DBCA. Finally we discussed renaming a PDB from the command line prompt. We have covered a lot of ground here, but these are not the only ways of getting PDB's into a CDB. Later in this book we will discuss plugging PDB's into a CDB and unplugging PDB's from a CDB. Next up though, we will discuss administration activities that are new to Multitenant databases.

Note!

There is one additional feature for creating clone PDB's that I didn't mention in this chapter, or in this book for that matter. This is a feature called CloneDB. This feature provides the ability to create clones quickly, using copy on write technologies. Rest assured that I will be covering CloneDB in book two of this series.

4
ADMINISTRATOIN OF CDB AND PDB DATABASES

There are several things you will want to know about the administration of CDB and PDB databases. In many ways the administration of both the CDB and its PDB's is not that far removed from what you are used to already. In this section we will discuss the following topics:

- Environmental information and views
- Managing the state of CDBs and PDBs
- Setting global storage limits on PDBs
- Create and remove tablespaces in PDBs
- Using the **alter system** and **alter session** commands in a Multitenant database.
- Managing temporary tablespaces
- Using Catcon.pl
- Using **_datafile_write_errors_crash_instance**

So, let's move onto the first topic!

Administration of CDBs and PDBs

In this section we will discuss the various administrative tasks that you might need to perform on CDBs and PDBs that are unique to Multitenant database. First we will take a quick look at some of the data dictionary views that you will use to manage a Multitenant database. Later in this book we will look at the data dictionary in more detail, including where various metadata is stored. Let's get with it!

Environment Information and Views Associated with Multitenant Databases

DBAs use various views, environmental variables, and commands to manage the Oracle Database. With Oracle Multitenant databases there is a host of new functionality introduced to support Multitenant database. This includes changes to the **sys_context** package, new **show** command in SQL*Plus and new and changed data dictionary views. We will discuss all these features in this section! Let's carry on.!

Environmental Information via sys_context

Within a CDB we have already indicated that each PDB has a container ID assigned to it. You can see the container ID in the V$CONTAINERS or V$PDBS view as seen in this example:

```
SQL> select con_id, name from v$pdbs;

    CON_ID NAME
---------- ------------------------------
         2 PDB$SEED
         3 ROBERTPDB
         4 TPLUG
         5 NEWPDB

SQL> select con_id, name from v$containers;

    CON_ID NAME
---------- ------------------------------
         1 CDB$ROOT
         2 PDB$SEED
         3 ROBERTPDB
         4 TPLUG
         5 NEWPDB
```

With that many containers you will probably agree that there is can be a lot of confusion when working in that environment. When you perform activities in a given PDB you will want to make sure you are in the correct PDB. If you are in SQL*Plus you can use the SQL*Plus built in commands **show con_name** and **show con_id** to see which container you are in and it's container id as seen in this example:

```
SQL> show con_name
CON_NAME
----------------------
NEWPDB

SQL> show con_id
CON_ID
----------------------
5
```

In this case we can see that we are in the NEWPDB PDB and the container ID is 5. You can also derive this information in PL/SQL through a call to **sys_context**. The standard namespace that contains the user environment settings (USERENV) has new parameters that are associated with Multitenant database. Table 4-1 provides a list of the **sys_context** Attributes that are associated with Multitenant databases.

Table 4-1 Sys_context Attributes for Multitenant

Attribute	Description
CDB_NAME	Returns the name of the CDB
CON_ID	Returns the ID of the container you were in
CON_NAME	Returns the name of the container
ORACLE_HOME	Returns the ORACLE_HOME setting

Here is an example of a query that calls the **sys_context** function returning the name of the container you are currently in:

```
SQL> Select sys_context('USERENV', 'CON_NAME') from dual;

SYS_CONTEXT('USERENV','CON_NAME')
-----------------------------------------------------------
NEWPDB
```

Exposing your Multitenant Environment Using SQL*Plus

Oracle has added new features to SQL*Plus that will help you as you navigate through the various containers in your database. Knowing these commands will help you to effectively navigate the PDB environment. You can see the list of these new commands in table 4-2.

Table 4-2 SQL*Plus Commands Associated with Multitenant

Command	Purpose
show con_id	Displays the container id (a numeric values) of the container that you are in.
show con_name	Displays the name of the container that you are currently in.
Show pdbs	Displays the PDB's in the CDB and their current state.

In this example we will demonstrate the use of the **show con_name** and **show pdbs** command from SQL*PLUS:

```
SQL> show con_name

CON_NAME
------------------------------
CDB$ROOT
```

```
SQL> show pdbs

CON_ID CON_NAME                        OPEN MODE   RESTRICTED
------ ------------------------------- ----------- ----------
     2 PDB$SEED                        READ ONLY   NO
     3 ROBERTPDB                       MOUNTED
     4 TPLUG                           READ WRITE  NO
     5 NEWPDB                          READ WRITE  YES
```

Using Database Views Related to Multitenant

There are some things that are different in the data dictionary views of a CDB. Also, there are data dictionary views that you will want to be aware of as you manage a Multitenant database. In this section we will look at the data dictionary and data dictionary views in more detail. First we will look at the changes in the data dictionary views related to Multitenant databases and their purpose and scope. Then we will take a quick look at views you will want to be aware of in a Multitenant database.

First, you will notice that many of the V$ data dictionary views that you are already familiar with, like V$TABLESPACE now have a new column called CON_ID. This column represents the container that the record belongs too. For example, look at the partial output from this query:

```
select a.con_id, a.name, b.name
from v$tablespace a, v$pdbs b
where a.con_id=b.con_id order by 1;
```

```
    CON_ID NAME                            NAME
--------- ------------------------------- --------------------
         2 TEMP                            PDB$SEED
         2 SYSAUX                          PDB$SEED
         2 SYSTEM                          PDB$SEED
         3 TEMP                            ROBERTPDB
         3 SYSAUX                          ROBERTPDB
         3 USERS                           ROBERTPDB
         3 SYSTEM                          ROBERTPDB
         4 TESTING2                        TPLUG
         4 TESTING                         TPLUG
         4 SYSAUX                          TPLUG
         4 SYSTEM                          TPLUG
         4 USERS                           TPLUG
         4 TEMP                            TPLUG
         5 SYSTEM                          NEWPDB
         5 SYSAUX                          NEWPDB
         5 TEMP                            NEWPDB
```

As you can see the NEWPDB PDB is assigned to CON_ID 5. You can see that there are 3 tablespaces assigned to the NEWPDB PDB. The DBA, USER and ALL views do not have this additional column in them in most cases. There are a few new views that contain the container ID in them, but the vast majority do not. The data contained in the DBA, USER and ALL views is dependent on which PDB you are logged into. If you are in the ROOT container, then all you will see is information related to the ROOT container. If you are in a PDB called TEST then you will only see the objects in the TEST PDB. Here is an example:

```
SQL> select count(*) from dba_tables;

  COUNT(*)
----------
      2340

SQL> alter session set container=newpdb;
Session altered.

SQL> select count(*) from dba_tables;
  COUNT(*)
----------
      2338
```

Notice the difference between these two queries. The first one shows that there are 2340 rows in the DBA_TABLES view in the ROOT container. The second query shows that there are 2338 tables in the NEWPDB container. This demonstrates the scope of the DBA, USER and ALL views is limited to the container that you are logged into.

However, a new kind of data dictionary view, called the CDB_ view has been added and it does contain the container ID for the objects in the database. For example, there is a CDB_TABLES view. Since we are still in the NEWPDB container, let's look at a **select count(*)** from that view:

```
SQL> select count(*) from cdb_tables;

  COUNT(*)
----------
      2338
```

Now, let's move back into the ROOT container and see what happens when we query the CDB_TABLES view:

```
SQL> show con_name
CON_NAME
------------------------------
CDB$ROOT
```

71

```
SQL> select count(*) from cdb_tables;

  COUNT(*)
----------
      4678
```

The reason that the CDB view shows so many more records here is that it contains the tables for all of the PDB's. This can be demonstrated by the following query:

```
SQL> select a.con_id, b.name, count(*)
  2  from cdb_tables a, v$containers b
  3  where a.con_id=b.con_id
  4* group by a.con_id, b.name;

    CON_ID NAME                                 COUNT(*)
---------- ------------------------------- ----------
         1 CDB$ROOT                             2340
         5 NEWPDB                               2338
```

Now, I know you are sharp and you noticed that only one PDB (and the ROOT container) is showing up in this view. That's because the CDB_TABLES view is only populated when the PDB is open either in READ ONLY or READ WRITE mode. So, the CDB views provide a look at PDB related objects to an administrator account logged into the ROOT PDB. In non ROOT PDBS the scope of the CDB views is only for that PDB. There is one additional twist to all of this and it's a user type that is new to Multitenant databases called a common user. We will discuss the common user, and about it's privileges, in the next chapter.

Oracle Database 12c Multitenant Specific Data Dictionary Views

Now that we have covered the scope of the various database views, it might be a good idea to give you a quick summary of the various views that are associated with Multitenant databases. Table 4-3 lists the most common V$ views that you will use to manage Multitenant databases. Table 4-4 below lists the most common DBA|ALL|USER_* views used to manage Multitenant databases. Also, don't forget that most of the DBA views have a related CDB_ view.

Table 4-3 Commonly Used V$ Views For Multitenant

View Name	Purpose
V$CONTAINERS	Contains information on the containers in the database including the ROOT and all PDBs.
V$PDB_INCARNATION	Provides information on incarnations specific to given PDBs.
V$PDBS	Provides information on PDBs within the database

Table 4-4 Commonly Used DBA|ALL and USER Views For Multitenant

View Name	Purpose
DBA_CONTAINER_DATA	Displays various container data for container data objects.
DBA_HIST_PDB_INSTANCE	Contains workload repository records for PDBs
DBA_PDB_HISTORY	Contains the history of a PDB. Only visible from within a specific PDB.
DBA_PDB_SAVED_STATES	Contains the saved state of a PDB. Managing the state of a PDB is discussed later in this section
DBA_PDBS	Contains a list of the PDBs in the database. Only visible from the ROOT container.
PDB_ALERTS	Provides information on specific PDB alerts.
PDB_PLUG_IN_VIOLATIONS	Provides information on incompatibilities between the CDB and the PDB.

The Data Dictionary CON_ID Column

We have already introduced you to the CON_ID column earlier in this book. Many of the data dictionary views have a new column called CON_ID added to them. The CON_ID column is used to identify the container (or PDB) that the row is associated with. For example if you look at the description of the V$TABLESPACE view you will see the CON_ID column that has been added in Oracle Database 12c as seen here:

```
SQL> desc v$tablespace
Name                                 Null?     Type
------------------------------       --------  -------------
TS#                                            NUMBER
NAME                                           VARCHAR2(30)
INCLUDED_IN_DATABASE_BACKUP                    VARCHAR2
BIGFILE                                        VARCHAR2
FLASHBACK_ON                                   VARCHAR2
ENCRYPT_IN_BACKUP                              VARCHAR2
CON_ID                                         NUMBER
```

The CON_ID column in the database views can be joined with the CON_ID column in the V$PDBS view to get the actual name of the container. Here is an example of a join between the V$TABLESPACE and V$PDBS view to see the name of a the tablespaces and the PDB's that they are assigned too:

```
SQL> select a.con_id, a.name, b.name
  2  from v$tablespace a, v$pdbs b
  3  where a.con_id=b.con_id
  4  Order by 1;

   CON_ID NAME                                    NAME
---------- ------------------------------------   ----------
        2 TEMP                                    PDB$SEED
        2 SYSAUX                                  PDB$SEED
        2 SYSTEM                                  PDB$SEED
        3 TEMP                                    ROBERTPDB
        3 SYSAUX                                  ROBERTPDB
        3 USERS                                   ROBERTPDB
        3 SYSTEM                                  ROBERTPDB
```

Managing the State of the CDB and it's PDBs

One of the basic DBA tasks is opening and closing a Multitenant database and it's CDBs. In this section we will discuss how to start and stop CDBs. Then we will look at opening and closing PDBs within a CDB.

Starting and Stopping the CDB

Starting and stopping a CDB is just like starting and stopping a non-Multitenant database. You simply use the SQL*Plus utility (or Oracle Enterprise Manager if you prefer) and issue the **startup** and **shutdown** commands as you always have. All of the same options still exist such as **startup force, shutdown abort** and **shutdown immediate**.

Starting and Stopping a PDB

There are three ways of starting and stopping a PDB. These are:

- Using the **alter pluggable database** command to startup and shutdown the PDB.
- Using the SQL*Plus **startup pluggable database** and **shutdown pluggable database** commands.
- Changing into the PDB you want to start or stop and issuing the SQL*Plus **startup** or **shutdown** command.

Let's look at each of these in more detail next.

Using the Alter Pluggable Database Command to Startup and Shutdown Databases

The **alter pluggable database** command can be used to startup and shutdown a pluggable database when logged into the CDB using the SYSDBA, SYSOPER, SYSBACKUP or SYSDG privileges. The **alter pluggable database** has a number of options to open a PDB with as seen in table 4-5 and a number of options to close a PDB in table 4-6. Each of the tables also has an example of the use of the option.

Table 4-5 Alter Pluggable Database Open Options

Option	Purpose	Example
Open (default)	Open the PDB in read write mode.	Alter pluggable database mypdb open;
Open read only	Open the PDB in read only mode.	Alter pluggable database mypdb open read only;
Open resetlogs	Open the PDB after a PITR.	Alter pluggable database mypdb open resetlogs;
Open restricted	Open the PDB in restricted mode.	Alter pluggable database mypdb open restricted;
Force	Force shutdown and restart	Alter pluggable database mypdb open force;
Upgrade	Open in upgrade mode	Alter pluggable database mypdb open upgrade;

Table 4-5 Alter Pluggable Database Close Options

Option	Purpose	Example
close (default)	Close the PDB normally	Alter pluggable database mypdb close;
Immediate	Force the PDB closed	Alter pluggable database mypdb close immediate;

Note!

We are deliberately not addressing RAC instances here. We will be addressing RAC and Oracle Multitenant in Book four.

*Using the SQL*Plus Startup and Shutdown Pluggable Database Commands*

You can use a version of the SQL*Plus **startup** and **shutdown** commands when connected to PDB's. You can use the SQL*Plus **startup** command to start a PDB when connected to the ROOT container or if you are connected to a PDB after using the **alter session set container** command. You must have the appropriate privileges (SYSDBA, SYSOPER, etc) to shutdown the pluggable database. Note that you cannot start a PDB by trying to connect to it through its service name. This is because the PDB is not registered with the listener until that PDB has been opened.

The options available with the **startup pluggable database** command can be seen in table 4-6. Note that in most cases the **open** option does not need to be included since it's the default value.

Table 4-6 Startup Pluggable Database SQL*Plus Commands

Option	Purpose	Example
Open (default)	Open the PDB normally	`Startup pluggable database mypdb`
Force	Force the PDB open	`Startup pluggable database mypdb force`
Upgrade	Open the PDB in upgrade mode	`Startup pluggable database mypdb upgrade`
Restricted	Open the PDB in restricted mode	`Startup pluggable database mypdb restricted`
Read only	Open the PDB in read only mode	`Startup pluggable database mypdb open read only`

*Using the SQL*Plus Startup and Shutdown Commands from within a PDB.*

The same options seen in Table 4-6 are available when using the SQL*Plus **startup** command when you are connected to the PDB. Since the PDB will be mounted, the only way to connect to it will be via the **alter session set container** command. Here is an example of connecting to a mounted PDB and starting it up with the SQL*Plus **startup** command:

```
SQL> alter session set container=newpdb;
Session altered.

SQL> startup
Pluggable Database opened.
```

There is not a **shutdown pluggable database** SQL*Plus command. However, the SQL*Plus **shutdown** command can be used on a PDB when you are connected to that PDB. The same commands available when shutting down a CDB are available when shutting down a PDB. These commands are seen in table 4-7 below:

Table 4-7 Shutdown SQL*Plus Commands for PDBs

Option	Purpose	Example
Normal (default)	Close the PDB normally, waiting for transactions to end and flushing all dirty blocks from the SGA.	**Shutdown**
Immediate	Close the PDB. Rollback any pending transaction. Flush the SGA.	**Shutdown immediate**
Abort	Shutdown the PDB without delay. Dirty buffers will be written to disk by the CDB if time allows.	**Shutdown abort**
Transactional	Shutdown the PDB after all active transactions have completed. Flush dirty buffers in the SGA to disk.	**Shutdown transactional**

Maintaining PDB State after CDB Restart

In Oracle Database 12.1.0.1 after a CDB was restarted, all of the PDB's would be in MOUNT mode. You would then need to manually open the PDB. Starting in 12.1.0.2 you can preserve the previous state of the PDB through a restart of the host CDB. This is done by using the **alter pluggable database save state** command when the PDB is in the state that you want it to be in when the CDB is restarted. You can see the saved state of the PDB using the DBA_PDB_SAVED_STATES view column STATE.

Let's look at an example of this. First, we are going to look at the saved state for the NEWPDB PDB by querying the DBA_PDB_SAVED_STATES view:

```
SQL> select a.name, b.state
  2  from v$pdbs a, dba_pdb_saved_states b
  3  where a.con_id=b.con_id;
no rows selected
```

The DBA_PDB_SAVED_STATES view is empty when a PDB has no state set for a given PDB. Now, let's look at the current state of the NEWPDB PDB:

```
SQL> select name, open_mode from v$pdbs;

NAME                              OPEN_MODE
------------------------------    ----------
PDB$SEED                          READ ONLY
ROBERTPDB                         MOUNTED
TPLUG                             MOUNTED
NEWPDB                            READ WRITE
```

So the NEWPDB PDB is open and in READ WRITE mode. Want to ensure that the NEWPDB returns to this mode if the CDB that the NEWPDB PDB is in restarted. So, we will use the **alter pluggable database save state** command to ensure the state of the PDB will be preserved across CDB restarts:

```
SQL> alter pluggable database newpdb save state;
Pluggable database altered.
```

Now, let's look at the DBA_PDBS_SAVED_STATES view again:

```
SQL> select a.name, b.state
  2  from v$pdbs a, cdb_pdb_saved_states b
  3  where a.con_id=b.con_id;

NAME                              STATE
------------------------------    -------------
NEWPDB                            OPEN
```

Now the current state of the NEWPDB PDB is saved and will be preserved across restarts of the parent CDB. Let's restart the CDB and see if this works:

```
SQL> shutdown abort
ORACLE instance shut down.
SQL> startup
ORACLE instance started.

Total System Global Area 2566914048 bytes
Fixed Size                  3048920 bytes
Variable Size             671091240 bytes
Database Buffers         1879048192 bytes
Redo Buffers               13725696 bytes
Database mounted.
Database opened.

SQL> select name, open_mode from v$pdbs;
NAME                             OPEN_MODE
------------------------------   ----------
PDB$SEED                         READ ONLY
ROBERTPDB                        MOUNTED
TPLUG                            MOUNTED
NEWPDB                           READ WRITE
```

You can see that the NEWPDB returned to READ WRITE mode after the database was restarted, just like we wanted.

To return to the default behavior for a PDB on a CDB restart, you will need to discard the saved state. This is done with the **alter pluggable database discard saved state** command. Here is an example where we return the NEWPDB PDB to the default state at CDB restart (which is MOUNTED). After resetting the state, notice that we no longer get any rows back when we query the DBA_PDB_SAVED_STATES view:

```
SQL> alter pluggable database newpdb discard state;
Pluggable database altered.

SQL> select a.name, b.state
  2  from v$pdbs a, dba_pdb_saved_states b
  3  where a.con_id=b.con_id;
no rows selected
```

Configuring Global Storage Limits for PDBs

Oracle Multitenant databases provide the ability to consolidate PDBs within the confines of a single instance. Each PDB can be managed by its own separate DBA who is isolated from all the other PDBs. Since each PDB can be managed independently, Oracle provides various controls that can be utilized to restrain resource usage within a given PDB. One of the constraints you can set on a PDB is how much overall physical disk space the tablespaces of a PDB can consume.

You can set the global storage limit on a PDB when it's created, by using the **pdb_storage_clause** clause of the **create pluggable database** command as seen in this example:

```
Create pluggable database mypdb
admin user robert identified by password role=(dba)
Storage (maxsize 20g);
```

To alter an existing storage limit or to define a new storage limit for a PDB you use the **pdb_storage_clause** clause along with the **alter pluggable database** command. To use this command you must be logged into the PDB with a user that has the alter database privilege. A common or local user of the PDB can be used to configure storage levels (we will discuss common and local users in the next chapter).

```
alter pluggable database mypdb storage (maxsize 30g);
```

An Oracle PDB can use one of two temporary tablespace types (we will discuss this in the next chapter). First, the CDB has a temporary tablespace that is common to the entire CDB. All PDB's can use this temporary tablespace, and by default all users in a PDB are assigned to that tablespace. If you are using a shared temporary tablespace, you can limit the amount of storage a PDB can consume in that tablespace by using the **pdb_storage_clause** either when creating a PDB or when using the **alter pluggable database** command. In this example, we are creating a PDB with storage limits on the CDB shared temporary tablespace:

```
Create pluggable database mypdb
admin user robert identified by password role=(dba)
Storage (maxsize 20g max_shared_temp_size 1g);
```

You can also use the **alter pluggable database** command to adjust or add storage limits on the shared temporary tablespace:

```
Alter pluggable database newpdb storage
(max_shared_temp_size 500m);
```

The default setting for these limits is for them to be unlimited. If you wish to return the storage settings to unlimited you can use the unlimited keyword to do so as seen in this example:

```
Alter pluggable database newpdb storage
(max_shared_temp_size unlimited);
```

Creating and Removing Tablespaces in a PDB

Since a PDB is just like an independent Oracle database, it makes sense that you can create tablespaces in that tablespace. The commands to create, alter or drop a tablespace in a PDB is just the same as the commands to perform these functions in a non-Multitenant database. The only difference is that the size of the datafiles in these tablespaces is limited by any restrictions at the PDB level on the total storage is can consume. For example, if we want to create a users tablespace that is 500MB then we would use the **create tablespace** command like this:

```
Create tablespace users datafile size 500m;
```

Dropping the tablespace is just the same too as seen here:

```
Drop tablespace users;
```

Other tablespace commands, such as those associated with resizing and adding datafiles work the same within a PDB as they do within the parent CDB or a non-Multitenant Oracle database.

Using the Alter System Command in a CDB and a PDB

There is no significant difference when the **alter system** command is executed from a CDB. The same privileges are required and the same restrictions apply. The only difference that is noticeable is that common users are used in a CDB and they are not even available in a non-Multitenant database. We will discuss common users in detail in the next chapter. All PDB's inherit the system settings from the CDB. These defaults can be over ridden by using the **scope=** parameter. Thus, you can set specific parameters for a PDB within an SPFILE so that they will be persistent.

There is a more limited list of **alter system** commands that can be used when you are connected to a PDB. To use the **alter system** commands you have the appropriate grants to use these commands. These privileges are the same as those required within a non-Multitenant database or a CDB. Table 4-8 lists the various **alter system** commands that can be run from within a PDB.

Table 4-8 List of Alter System Commands Available in a PDB

alter system flush shared_pool	alter system flush buffer_cache
alter system enable restricted session	alter system disable restricted session
alter system set use_stored_outlines	alter system suspend
alter system resume	alter system checkpoint
alter system check datafiles	alter system register
alter system kill session	alter system disconnect session

Like many other things, the **alter system** command's scope is limited to the PDB you are logged into. So, if you are logged into the MYPDB container, you can only kill sessions in the MYPDB container. Of course, if you are logged into the root as SYS or a common user, then you can kill any session.

Within a PDB, the **alter system set** command can modify parameters that have a setting of TRUE in the ISPDB_MODIFIABLE column of the V$SYSTEM_PARAMETER view. In version 12.1.0.2 there were over 180 system parameters that were modifiable at the PDB level. Almost 200 system parameters were not able to be modified in a PDB.

When you alter a system parameter you can save that parameter so that it's persistent across restarts of the PDB and its parent CDB. Thus, a given parameter can have multiple values across PDBs and the parent CDB. This can be seen by querying the V$SYSTEM_PARAMETER view as seen here:

```
SQL> select a.name pdb_name, b.name, b.con_id, b.value
  2  from v$system_parameter b,  v$containers a
  3  where a.con_id (+)=b.con_id
  4  and upper(b.name)='SESSIONS';


PDB_NAME   NAME          CON_ID VALUE
---------- ---------- ---------- ----------------
           sessions        0 472
```

Note!

The reason for the outer join is because the **V$CONTAINERS** view does not provide a row for CON_ID 0, which is the CON_ID for all the default parameters.

We can change the sessions parameter in the MYPDB PDB as seen here:

```
Alter session set sessions=100 scope=both;
```

Now we can re-issue the previous query and we will see that the value of the sessions parameter for the MYPDB PDB is different than the default:

```
SQL> select a.name pdb_name, b.name, b.con_id, b.value
  2  from v$system_parameter b,  v$containers a
  3  where a.con_id (+)=b.con_id
  4  and upper(b.name)='SESSIONS';
```

PDB_NAME	NAME	CON_ID	VALUE
MYPDB	sessions	6	100
	sessions	0	472

This parameter will persist through restarts of the PDB or the CDB.

Using the Alter Session Command in a CDB and a PDB

The **alter session** command can be used within a PDB or a CDB just as you do in a non-Multitenant database. You have already seen the use of the **alter session set container** command which provides the ability to move between containers when you are at the SQL prompt. All of the parameters related with the **alter session set** command are available within a PDB.

Temporary Tablespaces in a Multitenant Database

When a CDB is created, it will be created with its own temporary tablespace. When you create a PDB from the SEED database using the create pluggable database, a default temporary tablespace will be created in that pluggable database. All users who are created in the CDB (common users) or it's PDB's will be assigned the default temporary tablespace when they are created.

In early Oracle documentation in the past there was some reference to the ability of a PDB to share the CDB's temporary tablespace as a common temporary tablespace. There are many references to this on the internet as well. In 12.1.0.2 this functionality is not available nor was it documented at the time this book was written.

Every CDB and PDB has a default temporary tablespace assigned when it's created. When the CDB is created by the DBCA, or the PDB is created by the DBCA or the create pluggable database command, a default temporary tablespace will be created. The name of this tablespace is TEMP. You can see the setting of the default temporary tablespace by querying the DATABASE_PROPERTIES view and looking for the PROPERTY_NAME called DEFAULT_TEMP_TABLESPACE. Here is an example of such a query:

```
SQL> select PROPERTY_NAME, PROPERTY_VALUE
  2   from database_properties
  3   where upper(PROPERTY_NAME) like '%TEMP%';

PROPERTY_NAME                      PROPERTY_VALUE
--------------------------------   ----------------
DEFAULT_TEMP_TABLESPACE            TEMP
```

When a user is created in the CDB or PDB it will be assigned to the defined default temporary tablespace if one is not otherwise specified.

Management of temporary tablespaces and configuration of default temporary tablespaces in a CDB and its PDBs is the same as it is in non-Multitenant databases, so we will not spend time covering this functionality further.

The catcon.pl Script

Oracle Database 12c comes with a new perl script called catcon.pl. The purpose of this script is to provide the ability to run a given SQL script across multiple PDBs at the same time. Scripts run by catcon.pl can be run in a specific order and also you can define which PDBs the script will, and will not, be executed in. This script will be used in the future during database patching and upgrades to run upgrade scripts across all PDBs easily. This new script also produces output as the scripts are run and you can review this output afterwards.

Let's look at a simple example first. Let's assume you have the following script that you wish to run in all of the containers of the database. The script, in this case, sets the parameter sessions to 600 in all containers. The script is an easy, single line script that we will put into a SQL file called set_sessions.sql. We will save this file to a directory called $ORACLE_BASE/scripts. Here is the single line of the script:

```
Alter system set sessions=400 scope=both;
```

Now that we have created the script, we want to use catcon.pl to run it in all of the containers of the database. The command to do so looks like this:

```
$ORACLE_HOME/bin/perl $ORACLE_HOME/rdbms/admin/catcon.pl -d
$ORACLE_BASE/scripts -b /tmp/sessions_out sessions.sql
```

The result of the script above is that the sessions.sql script that is contained in the $ORACLE_BASE/script directory first in the root container, and then in the remaining containers. The catcon.pl script creates log files of its operations for review afterwards to ensure no errors have occurred. The catcon.pl script offers a number of different options that are available that make catcon.pl quite flexible. For example, you can have the catcon.pl run a SQL statement from the command line itself as seen here:

```
[oracle@bigdatalite ~]$ $ORACLE_HOME/perl/bin/perl
$ORACLE_HOME/rdbms/admin/catcon.pl -u SYS -e -b
/tmp/sessions_out -- --x"select * from dual"
catcon: ALL catcon-related output will be written to
/tmp/sessions_out_catcon_7706.lst
catcon: See /tmp/sessions_out*.log files for output
generated by scripts
catcon: See /tmp/sessions_out_*.lst files for spool files,
if any
Enter Password:
catcon.pl: completed successfully
```

Once the catcon.pl code has completed running you will find a variety of logs in the /tmp directory that start with the name sessions_out and then end with unique identifiers to keep the logs unique. The file name convention is platform specific. In these logs you will find the results of the scripts that were run, or in the case of the example above you will see the results of the query that was executed.

> **Note!**

At the time this book was written the Oracle documentation indicates that you should use single quotes instead of double quotes. In our testing, the statement required double quotes as we have used in our examples.

Avoiding CDB Crashes

If you have ever run into corruption issues with database datafiles you know that they can be a pain. However, very often the errors are localized to just a few blocks, and in a non-Multitenant database environment the database will continue to run normally. The offending datafile usually would be taken offline or sometimes it would remain online and users would only see errors when their process reads those bad blocks.

In Oracle Database 12c, the current default behavior if a PDB has any number of disk related errors, it will crash the entire CDB rather than just impacting the PDB itself. This is probably not the behavior that most enterprises want out of a Multitenant environment. To address this issue you can set the parameter _datafile_write_errors_crash_instance to a value of FALSE. The default value for this parameter is TRUE. You can see the current value of this parameter in your instance by running this query:

```
SELECT a.con_id container_id, a.ksppinm Param ,
b.ksppstvl SnVal , c.ksppstvl CDBVal
FROM x$ksppi a ,x$ksppcv b ,x$ksppsv c
WHERE
a.indx = b.indx AND
a.indx = c.indx AND
a.ksppinm LIKE '%_datafile_write_errors_crash_instance%'
ORDER BY 1,2;

CON_ID PARAM                                         SNVAL CDBVAL
------ --------------------------------------------- ----- ------
1      _datafile_write_errors_crash_instance         TRUE  TRUE
```

To reset the parameter you use the **alter system** command as seen here:

```
alter system set
"_datafile_write_errors_crash_instance"=FALSE scope=spfile;
```

Summary

We have covered a lot of ground in this chapter. We started by discussing how to get information on your Multitenant database with the data dictionary, the **sys_context** package and the SQL*Plus **show** command. We also talked about how to open and close CDBs and PDBs as well as managing the state of a PDB when a CDB is restarted. We then talked about setting storage limits, creating and removing tablespaces in a PDB, and using the **alter system** and **alter session** commands.

Then we finished off the chapter by discussing temporary tablespaces in a CDB/PDB, the new catcon.pl script and finally we talked about the hidden parameter **_datafile_write_crash_errors_on_instance** and how to use it to make sure your CDB does not crash should a PDB return a write error on a datafile operation.

This has been an important chapter as we really got into the meat of managing a Multitenant database. In the next chapter we will address users and security in a Multitenant database. Perhaps it is in that area that the largest number of impactful change to Oracle Database have occurred.

5
BASIC USER ADMINISTRATION AND SECURITY OF MULTITENANT DATABASES

The security architectures in a Multitenant databases is similar to that in a non-Multitenant database with a few additional wrinkles. The same basics apply that you are already familiar with. User access is facilitated with user accounts. These accounts are associated with schemas that own objects created by these users. User accounts are granted system level grants to facilitate system level privileges (ie: create session). When objects are created then object grants are assigned to various users, allowing them various forms of access to these objects. Roles are available to facilitate the easy granting of multiple privileges of system or object level grants. All of these things you are familiar remain the same.

There are some differences though, and we will focus on some of these differences in this chapter. First we will look at the additional types of users that you need to be aware of in Multitenant databases. For each user, we will look at their purpose, how to create them, and we will also look at the security concerns related to those kinds of users.

Users in the Multitenant Environment

There are some differences with respect to users in a Multitenant environment. In this section we will address those differences. First we will cover the basic user and security architecture of a Multitenant database. Then we will discuss a new type of user, the common users, that is available in a Multitenant database. We will also discuss system and object grants and how they work with common users. Then we will look at local users within a PDB and how to use them.

Multitenant User/Security Architecture Overview

The user and security architecture of a Multitenant database is slightly different but also very familiar. In a Multitenant environment we have new tiers of security to consider. First tier is at the CDB level and the second tier is at the PDB level. At both levels we still have the SYS account that can be used to manage overall CDB configurations as well as PDB configurations. As always, the SYS account is a super-user account and access to that account should be restricted as appropriate.

In non-Multitenant databases, it is common to create new accounts for individual DBA's or applications that have the privileges needed to manage a database. These accounts are often granted the DBA role, and some are granted the SYSDBA, SYSOPER, SYSBACKUP or other like privileges. This allows you to scope DBA level accounts to specific responsibilities.

In a Multitenant database, you cannot create normal user accounts when connected to the root of the CDB. For example, let's say I wanted to create an account called dbargf while connected to the root of a CDB called NEWPDB. This attempt will fail as seen here:

```
SQL> show con_name

CON_NAME
------------------------------
CDB$ROOT
SQL> create user dbargf identified by robert;
create user dbargf identified by robert
                   *
ERROR at line 1:
ORA-65096: invalid common user or role name
```

Of course, we don't want to use the SYS account every time we need to manage the CDB. So, can we create accounts that can be used to manage some of all functions of the CDB? Also, we know that accounts in PDB's are local to that PDB. Rather than creating the same account in fifteen different PDB's, is there a way to create one common account that is created in all of the PDB's? The answer is yes and the name of that account is the Common User Account.

With a Common User Account we can create a sort of global account. Like other Oracle accounts, the common user account has no privileges when it's created. Through the assignment of system and object grants and also the use of roles, we can assign privileges in a very granular way, just as with normal database accounts. Only, in the cast of Common User Accounts, the user account can have privileges granted in any PDB, across PDB's and in the CDB itself. It can become, in essence, a CDB super user account, if that is your wish.

In this section we will discuss common user accounts and how they are used in a Multitenant database. We will also discuss how to configure them for CDB management purposes.

Remember that in the CDB model, the individual PDBs are isolated from each other. All accounts created when connected to a PDB then is only related to that PDB. This is true for normal user accounts and privileged user accounts.

This provides the ability to isolate administration of individual PDB's to specific PDB administrative accounts. These kinds of accounts are called local administrator accounts. Users that are created locally within a PDB are called local users.

Common Users and Roles

As we mentioned in the previous section, you cannot create a normal "user" account when connected to the root container of a CDB. Instead we create accounts called common user accounts in the CDB. In this section we will first look at how to create a common user. Most of this discussion also applies to the creation and security aspects of roles as well. Where there is a difference, I will highlight that difference.

From the point of view of division of responsibilities the typical security model in a CDB is to have few CDB administrators and have the majority of administration activities occur at the PDB level. This allows you to DBAs to their various databases without a need to over allocate access to these DBA accounts.

In the next sections we will cover the creation of common users. We will then discuss the various ways you can grant privileges to common users after they have been created.

Creating and Removing Common Users

In a Multitenant database the ROOT container is special. It is the owner of all other PDBs within the database. You can access the ROOT container by using the standard Oracle database accounts like SYS (as sysdba) and SYSTEM (with or without SYSDBA) or you can create new accounts. However, you cannot create just any account when you are connected to the root container. Instead, you must create what is known as a *common user account*.

When it's created, the common user account is created in both the CDB and it's also created in all PDB's that are in the database. If a PDB is not open when the common user account is created, then the account will be created when the PDB is later opened. New PDB's that are plugged into the CDB will have the common user account added to them when they are plugged in.

Even though the common user account is created in all PDB's, it has no privileges anywhere by default. Therefore, nobody can use a common user account until it is granted privileges needed for whatever access is required.

The common user accounts can be used in a number of different ways. You can create common user accounts for your DBA staff, granting those accounts privileges only to the PDB's a given DBA would administer. This way, you can have DBA's who administer only specific PDB's and who do not have the ability to administer the CDB as a whole. Another example might be the creation of a common user account that is granted privileges to be able to backup the database, but nothing else.

A common user account has a special format to its name. The common user account name is identified by a prefix which is followed by the account name. By default, the prefix of a common user account is C##. So, if I wanted to create a common user account called dbargf I would actually create an account called C##dbargf as seen in this example:

```
SQL> create user c##dbargf identified by robert;
User created.
```

Once this common user is created, it's just like any other account – it lacks privileges of any kind. For example, if we try to log into the new c##dbargf account we get a familiar error:

```
ERROR:
ORA-01045: user C##DBARGF lacks CREATE SESSION privilege;
logon denied
```

As you can see, just like a regular user account, a common user account needs to be granted privileges like any other user account you might create. Let's look at how we grant privileges in the ROOT container to a common user account next.

You can drop a common user with the **drop user** command as seen here:

```
SQL> drop user c##dbargf;
```

Common Roles

Just like you can create a common user, you can also create a common role. The concept is the same. The role is created in all of the PDB's, but the privileges granted to that common role is granular to the level of the PDB (or CDB).

Creation of a common role is the same. The common role name begins with a C## prefix, just like a common user. Here is an example of the creation of a common role:

```
Create role c##crole identified by robert;
```

Now that we can create a common user or common role, we need to be able to grant privileges to them. There are two different situations we want to address with respect to granting privileges to common user accounts. The first is when you are logged into the ROOT container and you grant privileges to the common user from within the ROOT container. The second situation is granting privileges to a common user from within a PDB. Let's look at these two situations next.

Granting Privileges to the Common User (or Role) When Connected to the ROOT Container

In this section we will look at how you grant privileges (or roles) to common user accounts (or common roles). This is important since both common users and common roles have no privileges when they are created.

The types of privileges within a Multitenant database are the same as in the traditional non-Multitenant database. The first kind of privilege is the system privilege. These privileges provide access to system level commands. Examples of system privileges include commands such as the **alter session**, **create tablespace** and **create user** commands.

The second kind of privilege is an object privilege. These privileges provide specific access to database objects such as database tables. Any account that is created in a Multitenant database, including common accounts, must have privileges assigned before these accounts can actually do anything in the Multitenant database. Let's look at issuing both system and object level privileges when you are connected to the root container as a common user.

Granting Common Users System Grants within the ROOT Container

An example of a system privilege would be granting access to the ROOT container of the CDB. As with non-Multitenant databases, we grant the **create session** privilege to the account. To grant this privilege, you need to connect to the ROOT container with a privileged account such as the SYS user and use the **grant** command to enable the common user to log into the container.

In this example we connect to the container as SYS and issue the grant to provide the C##DBARGF privileges required to connect to the ROOT container.

```
SQL> connect / as sysdba
Connected.

SQL> grant create session to c##dbargf;
Grant succeeded.

SQL> connect c##dbargf/robert
Connected.
```

So, now we can connect to the CDB, but we still can't really do anything until we have granted additional privileges to the common user account, such as the DBA role.

Part of what the previous example demonstrates is that the granting of system and object grants is largely the same as with non-Multitenant databases. The same applies to roles, which can be used to group and classify a set of privileges (or other roles). By default, all privileges granted are scoped to the ROOT container only. By default, privileges granted to common accounts do not apply to that account within any PDB.

For example, if you grant the **alter session** system privilege to C##DBARGF and try to change into another container, you will receive an error because C##DBARGF has been granted no privileges in that container. Here is what such an error would look like:

```
SQL> alter session set container=newpdb;
ERROR:
ORA-01031: insufficient privileges
```

It is in this way that the isolation of PDB's is maintained (by default). The scope of all grants is limited to the container (or PDB) which they are granted. So, if you grant a privilege in the NEWPDB PDB, then that grant only has effect in the NEWPDB PDB.

This means that we need to look at how to grant common users access to PDBs, and perform actions in them. We will discuss that shortly.

Cascading ROOT Container System Privilege Grants to PDBs

Until now we have created a common user account. We have also granted it privileges within the ROOT container. Now, we want to extend this and grant the common user account we created system privileges in all PDB's. For example, we want the C##RGF account to be able to connect to any PDB after we have created that account. We can perform this grant, globally, from within the ROOT container.

To do this, we need to be connected into the ROOT container with an account that has already been granted one of two privileges:

- **grant any privilege**
- The privilege that is to be granted along with the **with admin option**

Again, this follows the same methods used in a non-Multitenant database.

For example, we created the C##DBARGF account earlier. Our intention is to use C##DBARGF is to use it as a common DBA account. We have decided to grant two system privileges to that account. These privileges are **create user** and **grant any privilege**. Here are the commands we would issue:

```
connect / as sysdba
grant grant any privilege to c##dbargf;
grant create user to c##dbargf;
```

This leads to an important point within a Multitenant database, and that is one of scope. When you issued the create user grant, the C##DBARGF account would seemingly be able to create users at that point. However, if you connect to the C##DBARGF account and try to create a user you will get the following error:

```
SQL>Connect c##dbargf/robert
connected.
SQL> create user c##dbanew identified by dbanew;
create user c##dbanew identified by dbanew
                                         *
ERROR at line 1:
ORA-01031: insufficient privileges
```

Why are we getting this error? The problem is one of scope. When you create a common user, remember that this user is created in every PDB within the database. You cannot create a common user that is only present in the ROOT container. This means that, while you are just issuing the **create user** command once, the practical result is that it's being cascaded through all of the PDBs. That leads to the problem we are facing. The default scope of any **grant** statement is to grant privileges in the current container only. Because we granted the **create user** privilege in the ROOT container, that grant only applies to that container. As soon as the **create**

user command cascades to create the common user in one of the PDBs it will fail because C##DBARGF does not have privileges to create a user in any of the PDBs of that database.

We solve this problem by adding the container clause to the **grant** command as seen here:

```
SQL>Connect / as sysdba
connected.
SQL> grant create session to c##dbargf container=all;
Grant succeeded.
```

Now, let's try that **create user** command again:

```
SQL> create user c##dbanew identified by dbanew;
User created.
```

Now it worked! This is important to remember when issuing system grants to common users, otherwise you might experience failures and wonder what went wrong.

Let's look at another example of privilege cascade. We have created the C##DBANEW user. Let's grant it the **create session** privilege and connect to the ROOT container using that account:

```
SQL> grant create session to c##dbanew;
Grant succeeded.
SQL> Connect c##dbanew/dbanew
Connected.
```

So good so far. What if we try to log into a PDB though? Here is what happens:

```
SQL> connect c##dbanew/dbanew@//minint-2hgbgqc:1522/newpdb
ERROR:
ORA-01045: user C##DBANEW lacks CREATE SESSION privilege;
logon denied
Warning: You are no longer connected to ORACLE.
```

Again, we can see that granting a privilege within the ROOT container only has effect in that container. Because we want to make sure the C##DBANEW account can connect to all PDBs then we need to scope of that grant be across the entire CDB. To do this we need to add the **container** clause to the **grant** statement. The container clause provides us with the ability to indicate what the scope of the **grant** command is. When you are in the ROOT container, there are two choices for the container clause. The first is the default, which is CURRENT. The second, which is optional, is ALL.

In this case, we will reissue the **create user** and **create session** grants, adding the **container=all** parameter. This will ensure both grants impact the all PDBs.

```
SQL> grant create session to c##dbanew container=all;
Grant succeeded.
SQL> grant create user to c##dbanew container=all;
Grant succeeded.
SQL> connect c##dbanew/dbanew@//minint-2hgbgqc:1522/newpdb
Connected.
```

After the execution of these grants, you can now connect to any PDB and create users within that PDB.

In some cases, such as the **create user** command, the **grant** command must include the **container=all** parameter. The default value for this clause from within the ROOT container is CURRENT. The need to use the **container=all** parameter is not required in most cases. In many cases, you may wish to limit a specific privilege to the ROOT container and one or more individual PDBs. In this case, you would issue the **grant** command in the ROOT container. Then you would log into the individual PDBs and grant the privilege to the common user from within that PDB. We will discuss granting privileges to a common user from inside of a PDB next.

Granting Common Users Object Grants within the ROOT Container

Granting object privileges to a user within the ROOT container should be a fairly rare thing. You should not be creating any objects in the ROOT container anyway. If you do need to grant object privileges, then the scope of those grants is constrained to the ROOT container only. You cannot grant object privileges on an object in a PDB to a common user from the ROOT container. These grants can only be done from within the PDB itself.

Granting Privileges to the Common User From Within PDBs

We have shown that you can grant a common user system level privileges to all PDBs when connected to the ROOT container of the PDB. However, there may be situations where you will want to grant a common user specific privileges that only apply in specific PDBs. In this case, you need to connect to the PDB and issue those grants from within the PDB itself.

Granting System Privileges to Common Users From Within PDBs

Earlier we granted **create session** privileges to the C##DBARGF common user from within the ROOT container. By default that privilege only allowed the common user to connect to the ROOT container. When we added the **container=all** parameter, then the common user was granted that privilege across all containers which allowed him to connect to any of the PDBs in the database. Neither of these is the perfect security solution. In most cases best practice would be to limit a common user to the specific PDBs that they need access too. For example assume I have a CDB which contains a set of PDBs for the HR application and another set of PDBs for the inventory application. I might want to create a common user for the DBA of the group of HR databases and grant that account the ability to connect to the HR databases. However, I might not want the DBA to be able to connect to the inventory databases.

To manage this level of security what you need to do is issue the **create session** system grant to the common user from within the PDB that you want the grant to apply too. In this case, we have a common user called C##HRDBA and we want to grant it access to the PDB called HR. What we will do is connect to the HR PDB using the admin user of that PDB. As you will recall, the admin user is defined in the **create pluggable database** command. Once we connect to the HR PDB, we will grant the C##HRDBA account the create session privilege so that it can connect to the PDB. We will then test the connection:

```
C:\Robert\logs>sqlplus robert/robert@//minint-
2hgbgqc:1522/hr
SQL*Plus: Release 12.1.0.2.0 Production on Sun Jan 18
15:08:26 2015
Copyright (c) 1982, 2014, Oracle.  All rights reserved.
Last Successful login time: Sun Jan 18 2015 15:06:31 -08:00
Connected to:
Oracle Database 12c Enterprise Edition Release 12.1.0.2.0 -
64bit Production
With the Partitioning, OLAP, Advanced Analytics and Real
Application Testing options
SQL> grant create session to c##hrdba;
Grant succeeded.
```

In this case, the C##HRDBA user can now log into the HR PDB. However, if it tries to log into another PDB that it has not been granted create session privileges on, the connection fails. Both cases are demonstrated here:

```
C:\Robert\logs>sqlplus c##hrdba/robert@//minint-
2hgbgqc:1522/hr
SQL*Plus: Release 12.1.0.2.0 Production on Sun Jan 18
15:12:56 2015
Copyright (c) 1982, 2014, Oracle.  All rights reserved.
Connected to:
Oracle Database 12c Enterprise Edition Release 12.1.0.2.0 -
64bit Production
With the Partitioning, OLAP, Advanced Analytics and Real
Application Testing options
SQL> quit
Disconnected from Oracle Database 12c Enterprise Edition
Release 12.1.0.2.0 - 64bit Production
With the Partitioning, OLAP, Advanced Analytics and Real
Application Testing options

C:\Robert\logs>sqlplus c##hrdba/robert@//minint-
2hgbgqc:1522/mypdb
SQL*Plus: Release 12.1.0.2.0 Production on Sun Jan 18
15:13:04 2015
Copyright (c) 1982, 2014, Oracle.  All rights reserved.
ERROR:
ORA-01045: user C##HRDBA lacks CREATE SESSION privilege;
logon denied
```

It is a best practice in most cases to grant specific system privileges to common users from the specific PDB rather than grant sweeping privileges that permit common users access to all of the PDBs in the database.

Granting Object Privileges to Common Users From Within PDBs

For example, say there is a table in the NEWPDB PDB called TESTING that was created by a local account (we will discuss local accounts later in this section) called ROBERT. We want to grant SELECT access to this table to the common user C##DBARGF, but we don't want to grant C##DBARGF sweeping system privileges like **select any table**. In this case, the owner of the object (ROBER) or a local PDB administrator would need to grant access to that object to the C##DBARGF common user. As an alternative they could grant access to a role (local or common) and then grant that role to the common user.

In this example, we first log into the NEWPDB PDB as a local user called ROBERT. The ROBERT user will create a table called TESTING. Then, the ROBERT user will grant the **select** privilege to the common user C##DBARGF account:

```
C:\Robert\logs>sqlplus robert/robert@//minint-
2hgbgqc:1522/newpdb
SQL*Plus: Release 12.1.0.2.0 Production
on Sun Jan 18 13:38:56 2015
Copyright (c) 1982, 2014, Oracle.  All rights reserved.
Last Successful login time: Sun Jan 18 2015 13:24:18 -08:00
Connected to:
Oracle Database 12c Enterprise Edition Release 12.1.0.2.0 -
64bit Production
With the Partitioning, OLAP, Advanced Analytics and Real
Application Testing options
SQL> create table testing (id number);
Table created.
SQL> grant select on testing to c##dbargf;
Grant succeeded.
```

Keep in mind that the TESTING table is owned by the ROBERT user. Also, note in this example that we didn't need to use the **container** clause when we issued the **grant** command. The **container** clause is really not valid when you are in a PDB – the only available option there is CURRENT.

Continuing our example, we connect to the NEWPDB PDB with the C##DBARGF account that we just provided **select** privileges on the ROBERT.TESTING table too. We then issue a **select** command to demonstrate that the C##DBARGF now has **select privileges** to that object:

```
C:\Robert\logs>sqlplus c##dbargf/robert@//minint-
2hgbgqc:1522/newpdb as sysdba
SQL*Plus: Release 12.1.0.2.0 Production on
Sun Jan 18 11:05:08 2015
Copyright (c) 1982, 2014, Oracle.  All rights reserved.
Connected to:
Oracle Database 12c Enterprise Edition Release 12.1.0.2.0 -
64bit Production
With the Partitioning, OLAP, Advanced Analytics and Real
Application Testing options

SQL> grant create session to C##dbargf;
Grant succeeded.
```

Now, the C##DBARGF account can connect to the NEWPDB PDB and query the ROBERT.TESTING table since it has access to that object now by virtue of the **select** grant issued to it. Here is an example where the C##DBARGF account is used to query that table:

```
C:\Robert\logs>sqlplus c##dbargf/robert@//minint-
2hgbgqc:1522/newpdb as sysdba
SQL*Plus: Release 12.1.0.2.0 Production on
Sun Jan 18 11:06:35 2015
Copyright (c) 1982, 2014, Oracle.  All rights reserved.
Connected to:
Oracle Database 12c Enterprise Edition Release 12.1.0.2.0 -
64bit Production
With the Partitioning, OLAP, Advanced Analytics and Real
Application Testing options
SQL> select * from robert.testing;
no rows selected
```

Recapping Grants

We have covered a lot of ground on both system and object grants to common users. It might be worthwhile to summarize the things we have covered. Table 5-1 provides a quick summary of the scope of a specific **grant** to an object, depending on where that grant occurred and if the **container** option has been used.

Table 5-1 Scope of Grant Commands on Common Users

Granted in PDB or ROOT	Grant Type	Container option?	Scope of grant
ROOT	SYSTEM	Not Used	Just the ROOT Container
ROOT	SYSTEM	YES	All PDBs without restriction
ROOT	OBJECT	NO	ROOT Container only. No global object grant from ROOT supported.
PDB	SYSTEM	NO	Just the PDB.
PDB	OBJECT	NO	Just the PDB

Local PDB Accounts

We have covered common user accounts which can be used to manage the CDB and any number of PDBs in a container database. Most accounts in a CDB database will not be common user accounts though, they will be local administrators or local user accounts. First we will look at local administrator accounts and then we will look at local user accounts.

Local Administrators

Given that the objective of a CDB is to keep all of its subject PDBs isolated from each other, it follows that each PDB must have its own set of local administrative accounts. This is further reinforced by the fact that the create pluggable database requires the definition of a admin account when it's used to create a PDB from the SEED container. Each PDB can have one or more administrator accounts. These accounts can be granted the system grants required to administer the PDB.

The most obvious local administration account in a PDB created from the SEED container is the admin account that is defined in the **create pluggable database** command. Even this administrative user has limited privileges when it's created. By default, when the admin user is created in a new PDB it has these privileges:

- **Unlimited tablespace**
- **Create pluggable database** (through a grant to the **pdb_dba role**)
- **Create session** (through a grant to the **pdb_dba role**)
- **Set container** (through a grant to the **pdb_dba role**)

So, while you can connect using the newly created PDB admin user, there isn't much you can do with it until you grant it additional privileges. You can use the **pdb_dba_roles** clause of the **create pluggable database** command to grant additional roles (such as DBA) to the admin user when you create the PDB, or you can log in afterwards as SYS and grant the admin user it's privileges.

Local Users
The local user in a PDB is just like a non-administrative user account in a non-Multitenant database. You create the accounts inside the PDB you want them assigned to by using the **create user** command. Once the user account is created you can administer privileges, create and delete objects, load and execute PL/SQL objects and any other activity that a normal user account would perform. The namespace for a user account name is limited to the PDB, so the same user account can exist in more than one PDB. This is very helpful for cloning purposes where you want to take an existing database and clone it to a newly created database.

Accessing Data Across PDBs
There will be cases where you will want to provide a user in one PDB the ability to access data in another PDB. In a non-PDB environment you would create a database link and access the remote data directly through that database link. The same technique can be used to access data across PDBs. For example, assume that I have two PDBs. One is called PDB1 and the other is called PDB2. Assume in PDB1 that we have a user called USER1. PDB1.USER1 has a table called SOURCE_TABLE.

Now, assume that in PDB2 we have a user called USER2. PDB2.USER2 has a need to access the data in the SOURCE_TABLE in the PDB1.USER1 PDB. To do this, we can create a database link between the two PDBs called TOUSER1. We will connect to the USER2 schema in the PDB2 PDB which we have already granted the privileges required to create a database link to PDB2.USER2. Then we will create a database link using the **create database link** command. This database link will point to the PDB1.USER1 schema, so we can query the SOURCE_TABLE table. Here is an example of this operation:

```
sqlplus USER2/robert@//minint-2hgbgqc:1522/pdb2

create database link touser1
connect to user1 identified by robert
using '//minint-2hgbgqc:1522/pdb1';

SQL> select count(*) from source_table@touser1;
  COUNT(*)
----------
         1
```

Another method of access data through a PDB is to use the containers clause which was introduced in Oracle Database 11.1.0.2. This features requires that you use a common user, and that the object to be queried is owned by that common user. Let's look at an example. We can look at the USER_USERS tables across the PDBS by issuing the following query. First, we have to be connected to the ROOT container. Then you issue the **select** statement using the **containers** clause:

```
Connect / as sysdba
Select count(*) from containers(user_users);
```

This query will cross all PDBs (including the root container) and generate a common count(*) for the USER_USERS views. Note that if you are not connected to the ROOT container the results you will get back will be for only the PDB you are connected too.

This cross PDB activity can be done for user created tables too. There are some pretty restrictive rules, however:

1. That you are connected to a common user.
2. You must be logged into the root container.
3. The table that you are going to query must be present in every container. There is an option to exclude PDBs from the query but the table must still be present in the excluded PDB.

Summary

In this chapter we have covered a lot of ground. We have discussed common users and how they are used in a Multitenant database. We have talked about how to create common users. We also discussed the various types of ways that common users have privileges granted to them. We then discussed local accounts, including local administrator and local user accounts. Finally we discussed how to share data between PDBs.

This is also the end of Book one of this series on Oracle Multitenant and I hope you liked it. Coming up in Part 2 is even more coverage on Oracle Multitenant databases. In Part Two we discuss:

- Plugging in and unplugging PDBs
- Plugging a non-CDB database into a CDB database as a PDB.
- Unplugging a PDB and turning it into a non-Multitenant database.
- Backup and restoring Multitenant databases.

Then, in Part Three we will provide even more coverage on Multitenant databases. In Part Three we will discuss:

- Monitoring a Multitenant database
- Performance tuning a Multitenant database
- Oracle Enterprise Manager and Multitenant databases
- Upgrading Multitenant databases.

Finally, in Part Four we will finish off this series by covering the following topics:

- Controlling Multitenant resources with resource manager
- Replication and Oracle Multitenant databases
- Using Oracle Data Guard with Multitenant databases
- Multitenant in a Real Applications Cluster environment

I hope you enjoyed this book and I hope you enjoy the rest of the series on Oracle Multitenant databases.

INDEX

ABOUT THE AUTHOR

Robert G. Freeman works in the Public Sector Group of the North American Sales Organization for Oracle Corp as an Oracle Database Expert. In this position he provides technical assistance for new and existing customers who are installing, upgrading or adding to existing database infrastructures. Robert has been working with Oracle Databases for over 25 years. He is the author of numerous books including Oracle Database 12*c* New Features, Oracle Database 12*c* RMAN Backup and Recovery and several other books. Robert lives in Las Vegas, NV. with his wonderful wife Carrie and his sixth child Amelia. Robert is the father of five other amazing children who are now five wonderful adults who he is very proud of.